Hong Hu
Liang Pang

Perception Granular Computing in Visual Cognition Task

Hong Hu
Liang Pang

Perception Granular Computing in Visual Cognition Task

LAP LAMBERT Academic Publishing

Impressum / Imprint

Bibliografische Information der Deutschen Nationalbibliothek: Die Deutsche Nationalbibliothek verzeichnet diese Publikation in der Deutschen Nationalbibliografie; detaillierte bibliografische Daten sind im Internet über http://dnb.d-nb.de abrufbar.

Alle in diesem Buch genannten Marken und Produktnamen unterliegen warenzeichen-, marken- oder patentrechtlichem Schutz bzw. sind Warenzeichen oder eingetragene Warenzeichen der jeweiligen Inhaber. Die Wiedergabe von Marken, Produktnamen, Gebrauchsnamen, Handelsnamen, Warenbezeichnungen u.s.w. in diesem Werk berechtigt auch ohne besondere Kennzeichnung nicht zu der Annahme, dass solche Namen im Sinne der Warenzeichen- und Markenschutzgesetzgebung als frei zu betrachten wären und daher von jedermann benutzt werden dürften.

Bibliographic information published by the Deutsche Nationalbibliothek: The Deutsche Nationalbibliothek lists this publication in the Deutsche Nationalbibliografie; detailed bibliographic data are available in the Internet at http://dnb.d-nb.de.

Any brand names and product names mentioned in this book are subject to trademark, brand or patent protection and are trademarks or registered trademarks of their respective holders. The use of brand names, product names, common names, trade names, product descriptions etc. even without a particular marking in this work is in no way to be construed to mean that such names may be regarded as unrestricted in respect of trademark and brand protection legislation and could thus be used by anyone.

Coverbild / Cover image: www.ingimage.com

Verlag / Publisher:
LAP LAMBERT Academic Publishing
ist ein Imprint der / is a trademark of
OmniScriptum GmbH & Co. KG
Heinrich-Böcking-Str. 6-8, 66121 Saarbrücken, Deutschland / Germany
Email: info@lap-publishing.com

Herstellung: siehe letzte Seite /
Printed at: see last page
ISBN: 978-3-659-74455-6

Zugl. / Approved by: Beijing, Institute of Computing Technology, CAS, 2015

Perception Granular Computing in Visual Cognition Task

Hong Hu, Liang Pang

Preface

The purpose of the book is to advance in the understanding of brain functions by defining a general framework for representation based on granular computing theory. The idea is to bring this mathematical formalism into the domain of fuzzy neural representation of visual cognition, setting the basis for a theory of image understanding and learning of visual tasks. In the past decade, granular computing (GrC) has been an active topic of research in machine learning and computer vision. However, the granularity division is itself an open and complex problem. Deep learning, at the same time, has been proposed by Geoffrey Hinton, which simulates the hierarchical structure of human brain, processes data from lower level to higher level and gradually composes more and more semantic concepts.

The information similarity, proximity and functionality constitute the key points in the original insight of granular computing proposed by Zadeh. The information similarity and proximity depended on the samples distribution can be easily described by the fuzzy logic. From this point of view, GrC can be considered as a set of fuzzy logical formulas, which is geometrically defined as a layered framework in a multi-scale granular system. The necessity of such kind multi-scale layered granular system can be supported by the columnar organization of the neocortex. A novel learning approach of granular system has been proposed in this book, which uses a hybrid method which combines fuzzy logical designing, PSVM and back propagation in the learning processing of a multi layered neural network. This novel approach gives a new focus to deep learning. For more, the granular system proposed in this book can be viewed as a new explanation of deep learning that simulates the hierarchical structure of human brain. In this book, we try to the concept of granular system to structuring design of deep learning.

Unlike those previous works on the theoretical framework of GrC, our granular system is abstracted from brain science and information science, and it can be embedded in a neural dynamical system, a simple way to complete this task is to design a layered dynamic neural network working as the way of granular computing in its static point. So it is helpful to guide designing of brain like computer for the tasks of image understanding. At other hand, in a complicate task of visual cognition, dynamic cooperation and competition in the interacting procedure of different substances, neuron cells, neural system structures are necessary. So how to design a dynamic granular system is also briefly discussed in this book. Finally, we take the task of image-matting as an example to demonstrate that our multi-scale GrC has high ability to increase the texture information entropy and improve the effect of object-background separating.

Contents

8 Discussion

Chapter 1

Introduction

To probe the mechanism of information processing in our brain is a marvelious and most attractive topic in artificial intelligence and cognition science. Unfortunately, the unimaginable complex of brain structure prevents our imitations of brain functions. It is necessary to develop a general framework for neural network representation and processing in the task of cognition. In this book, the framework of granular computing is introduced to bridge the gap between brain cognitive ability and neural network.

Lin T Y (2012) pointed out that Granulation seems to be a natural methodology deeply rooted in human thinking. Many daily things are routinely granulated into sub-things [43]. In the IEEE-GrC2006 conference of information about the granular computing (GrC), the outline of GrC is defined as a general computation theory for effectively using granules such as classes, clusters, subsets, groups and intervals to build an efficient computational model for complex applications with huge amounts of data, information and knowledge [3]. Just as the scholars summarized in the IEEE-GrC2006 conference though the label is relatively recent, the basic notions and principles of GrC, though under different names, have appeared in many related fields, such as information hiding in programming, granularity in artificial intelligence, divide and conquer in theoretical computer science, interval computing, cluster analysis, fuzzy and rough set theories, neutrosophic computing, quotient space theory, belief functions, machine learning, databases and many others [3]. The above definition of GrC is too augmental and the subjects about classes, clusters, subsets, groups and intervals have already studied by artificial intelligence and mathematics for a long time. So old version of Granular computing is just an abstraction of old methods.

What is really new point for GrC ? We think that the new or main point of the GrC lies in the original insight of GrC proposed by Zadeh, in which there are three basic concepts that underlie human cognition: granulation, organization and causation. Informally, granulation involves decomposition of whole into parts; organization involves integration of parts into whole; and causation involves association of causes with effects. Granulation of an object A leads to a collection of granules of A, with a granule being a clump of points (objects) drawn together by indistinguishability, similarity, proximity or functionality [70]. In this original insight of GrC, Zadel pointed out three important aspects about GrC :

(1) the GrC is a main character of human cognition;

(2) so called GrC is based on indistinguishability, similarity, proximity or functionality;

(3) there is a close relationship among granulation, organization and causation.

Based on these points, we think that it is necessary to find some key points of GrC in human cognition. There are two kinds of GrC research: perception-level and knowledge-level. A perception-level GrC does a series feature transformation and tries to find meta-knowledge implied in samples; a knowledge GrC tries to process knowledge or structure information based on metal-knowledge. In this book we focus on the perception-level.

Indistinguishability, similarity and proximity can be described by equivalence relation or tolerance relation, and these relations can be described by some kind distance functions. From the relevant literature, it is easy to see that many GrC researches focus on classification and clustering [62, 67, 71, 72]. Zhang et al. [71–74] use the quotient space theory to try to study indistinguishability and similarity. Yao [68] extends the equivalent class to rough approximation set. The quotient space structure described by equivalence relation is used to probe the structure of granules such as classes, clusters, subsets, groups etc. In a more general way, Lin [41, 44] and Yao [65, 66] use binary relations and neighborhood systems to study indistinguishability and similarity respectively, the geometric concepts: partitions, covering and topology, and neighborhood can be described by binary relations in the algebra. Pedrycz A et al.(2012) define granular on fuzzy sets and discuss several operations and their granular consistency [51]. Lin T Y(2012) [43] gives out a summary about the history of granular computing, he discusses all formal description of granular computing and some further directions e.g. GrC, databases and data mining, GrC and clouding computing etc.

In fact, GrC should be discussed in the framework of human cognition from perception to pattern recognition and knowledge processing. Although the concept of granular computing has been proposed more than ten years, only few people pay attention to this subject. In fact granular computing pays much more attention to the leveled computing of intelligence. Just as Yao Y.(2006) [63] pointed out:" Granules in the family are called focal elements of discussion at the level. Each level is represented by a plane. While granules at the same level are of similar nature, granules at different levels may be very different. Consequently, we may use different vocabularies and languages for descriptions at different levels."

The leveled computation revealed by granular computing is very important for machine learning. In this book, we show that such kind leveled computation can be described by a set of fuzzy logical functions. We theoretically proved that if the multi scale structure and input-output relation of a granular system can be described by a set of fuzzy logical functions, the granular computing on such kind granular system can be completed by a layered neural network with a sigmoid function as its nonlinear output function.

Nowadays the learning of multi layers' neural networks becomes a huge wave of technology trends for big data and artificial intelligence, e.g. the famous approach deep learning. The term deep learning gained much attraction in the mid-2000s after a publication by Geoffrey Hinton [28]. Deep learning simulates the hierarchical structure of human brain, processes data from lower level to higher level, and gradually composes more and more semantic concepts. These facts mean that deep learning has a close relationship with the granular computing.

All the granular computing researches aforementioned, in general, neglect information transformation and feature abstraction, which are very important for deep learning. In this book, we propose a novel learning approach of granular system, which uses a hybrids method which combines fuzzy logical designing, Proximal support vector machine (PSVM) and back propagation in the learning processing of a multi layered neural network, this novel approach gives a new focus to deep learning, and make the structure designing of deep learning under the help of fuzzy logic possible.

Driven by rapid ongoing advances in computer hardware, neuroscience and computer science, artificial brain research and development are blossoming [12]. The representative work is the Blue Brain Project, which has simulated about 1 million neurons in cortical columns and included considerable biological detail to reflect spatial structure, connectivity statistics and other neural properties [14]. The more recent work of a large-scale model for the functioning brain is reported in the famous journal Science, which is done by the group of Chris Eliasmith's group [15]. In order to bridge the gap between neural activity and biological function, Chris Eliasmith's group presented a 2.5-million-neuron model of the brain (called "Spaun") to exhibit many different behaviors. Among these large scale visual cortex simulations, the visual cortex simulations are most concerned. The two simulations aforementioned are all about the visual cortex. The number of neurons in cortex is enormous. According to [50], the total number in area 17 of the visual cortex of one hemisphere is close to 160,000,000. For the total cortical thickness the numerical density of synapses is 276,000,000 per mm^3 of tissue. It is almost impossible to design or analyze a neural network with more than 10^8 neurons only based on partial differential equations. The nonlinear complexity of a brain prevents our progress from simulating useful and versatile functions of our cortex system. Many studies only deal with simple neural networks with simple functions, and the connection matrices should be simplified. The visual functions simulated by "Blue Brain Project" and "Spaun" are so simple that they are nothing in the traditional pattern recognition.

On the other hand, logic inference plays a very important role in our cognition, with the help of logical design, the things become simple, and this is the reason why computer science has made a great progress. There are more than 10^8 transistors in a CPU today. Why don't we use similar techniques to build complex neural networks? The answer is yes.

As our brains work in the non Turing computable way, fuzzy logic rather than Boolean logic should be used. For this purpose, we introduce a new concept - fuzzy logical framework of a neural network. Fuzzy logic is not a new topic in science, but it is really very fundamental and useful. If the function of a dynamical neural network can be described by fuzzy logical formulas, it can greatly help us to understand behavior of this neural network and design it easily.

For neural systems, the basic logic processing module to be used as a building module in the logic architectures of the neural network comes from OR/AND neuron [29,53], also referred by [34]. The ideal of hybrid design neural networks and fuzzy logical system is firstly proposed by [40]. While neural networks and fuzzy logic have added a new dimension to many engineering fields of study, their weaknesses have not been overlooked, in many applications the training of a neural network requires a large amount of iterative calculations. Sometimes the network cannot adequately learn the desired function. Fuzzy systems, on the other hand, are easy to understand because they mimic human thinking and acquire their knowledge from an expert who encodes his knowledge in a series of if/then rules [52].

Neural networks can work either in dynamical way or static way. The former can be described by partial differential equations and denoted as "dynamical neural networks". Static points or stable states are very important for dynamical analysis of a neural network. Many artificial neural networks are just abstract of static points or stable states of dynamical neural networks, e.g. perception neural networks, such kind artificial neural networks work in a static way and are denoted as "static neural networks". We proved that leveled granular computing can be taken place in a layered static neural network, so there is a natural relation between a static neural network and a fuzzy logical system. But for dynamical neural networks, we should extend the static fuzzy logic to dynamic fuzzy logic. In this book, we also briefly discuss the problem of how to design a dynamical neural network system for simulation of visual cognition processing. Usually, a dynamical neural network can be designed by composing several layered neural networks, so in this book, we focus on the topic of how to design layered neural networks which work in the static way. At last of our book, a concrete granular system has been built for the purpose of information transformation and object-background separation. We take the image matting task as an example to validate the ability of our granular system.

The main contributions of this book include:

(1). In this book, we try to to make a structure designing of layered deep learning by abstracting the complicate processing of visual perception to a novel and simply described model, such kind model is denoted as " granular computing", and has a multi scale layered structure from feature abstraction to classification;

(2).Our novel granular system has a close relation with deep learning, so it develops a new focus for deep learning. It is the first time that fuzzy logic is introduced for leveled feature abstraction in deep learning ;

(3).Although fussy logic is often mentioned in granular computing, for example,fuzzy logic and rough set technique are used by Lin T Y (1999) [42] for word computing, and Liu H et al.(2012) use fuzzy lattices in the classification based on hyper spherical granular computing [45]. In this book ,fuzzy logic is not only used for describing granular similar to hyper spherical granular in [45], but also for feature abstraction and classification. For this purpose, we propose a novel and effective approach which is combined fuzzy logical designing, PSVM [18] and back propagation;

(4). We also probe the problem about the relationship of a fuzzy logical system and a dynamical neural system;

(5). The granular computing proposed by us gives a novel approach for the task of image-matting, the experiments' result show that this approach is sound.

The rest of this book is organized as follows: the chapter 2,introduces the basic concept of granular system based on tolerance relation; the chapter 3 analyzes the relation of logistical function and fuzzy logic at first, then proposes an novel approach to design leveled perception granular system by hybrid fuzzy logical design and learning algorithms of perception leveled neural network; the chapter 4 probes the problem of granular computing in the static state of a layered dynamical neural system and answered the question of the possibility of simulating fuzzy granular computing in a layered dynamical neural networks by proving three important theorems; the chapter 5 probes the problem of how to design dynamic neural system; the chapter 6 gives out formal definition of a granular system for visual task; the chapter 7 discusses the application of perception granular system in the image matting task, the experiments' results are showed in this section; the last chapter 8 is the discussion and looking forward to the future.

Notation in this book: If no explicit declaration, we use the bold italic uppercase characters to represent function set $\boldsymbol{F}$, the italic uppercase characters to represent vector function F , italic lowercase characters to represent scale function f, decorated letter of bold uppercase characters to represent vector set or matrix $\mathbb{X}$, bold uppercase characters to represent scale real values set, e.g. whole real values' set $\mathbb{R}$, the n-dimensional real vectors'set is denoted as "$\mathbb{R}^n$". uppercase characters to represent vectors X, and lowercase characters to represent scale values.

The training samples set is denoted as $\mathbb{X} = [\mathbb{X}_0, \mathbb{X}_1]$, here the $n \times m_i$ matrix $\mathbb{X}_i = \{X_{i,1}, X_{i,2}, \cdots, X_{i,m_i}\}$ is the training samples matrix of the class $i, (i = 0, 1)$, and $X_{i,j}^T = [x_{i,j,1}, x_{i,j,2}, , x_{i,j,n}]$ is the jth training sample of the class i.

Chapter 2

Granular System Based on Tolerance Relation

The difference between a granular system based on equivalence relation and a granular system based on tolerance relation is that an equivalence relation will divide a space into nonoverlapping covering while a tolerance relation will create overlapping covering of this space.

Yiyu Yao (2013)et al. proposed granular computing paradigm for concept learning in which two learning strategies are investigated. A global attribute-oriented strategy searches for a good partition of a universe of objects and a local attribute-value-oriented strategy searches for a good covering [64]. In this book, granular computing is started from feature vectors e.g. images, not attributes. In order to simulation perception procession of our cognition, we define a set of multi-scale nested convex regions with a corresponding computing based on this set . There are two main purposes to build such a granular system based on tolerance relation:

1. Granular systems are designed to describe similarity and proximity of information, which can be described by tolerance relation. Granular systems based on tolerance relation can be viewed as a topological structure built by topological bases on the topological space $(\mathbb{X}, \tau)$ induced from a metric space $(\mathbb{X}, dis)$ by the metric dis. Granular systems based on tolerance relation can be used to describe domain stricture, which represents indistinguishability, similarity and proximity of examples.Classification is determined by the indistinguishability, similarity and proximity of information.

There are two kind similarity among examples-static similarity and dynamical similarity.

(a).If elements of classes are distributed in standard convex regions, we can use some kind distance function to describe classes distribution domains. In this case, similarity between two objects can be intuitively described by distance functions. If $dis(X, Y)$ is a distance function in the n-dimensional space $\mathbb{R}^n$ and C is a point in $\mathbb{R}^n$, the formula $dis(C, Y) < r$ described a convex region $\mathbb{D}$ in $\mathbb{R}^n$ which takes C as its center.

Every point Y in this region is equal to $Y = C + E$, here E is some kind noise, if $\mathbb{D}$ is just a ball, E can be viewed as white noise which has an amplitude less than r. We denote such kind similarity as static similarity.

(b). The dynamical similarity is different from static similarity, if one object O_1 continuously changes to another object O_2, e.g. a tadpole continuously grow up to a frog, then O_1 and O_2 are dynamical similar, i.e. if all elements in a class A are dynamical similar, the distribution domain of A is a connected domain. Dynamical similarity will cause distribution domain become very complicate and have a nonlinear borderline. Although,a dynamical similarity may cause the inner class difference larger than the among classes difference, it can also be described by equivalence relation or tolerance relation. The difference of a granular system based equivalence relation and granular system based on tolerance relation is that an equivalence relation will divide a space into non overlapping covering and a tolerance relation will create overlapping covering of this space. The relation described by the formula $dis(X, Y) < r$ is the special case of a tolerance relation.

2. The main purpose of information transformation in pattern recognition is to recognize or classify different objects from their mixtures, so information transformation used in pattern recognition should be taken place in a granular system which describes static similarity and dynamical similarity. This is the main point we will discuss in this book.

Similarity can be described by fuzzy logical formula based on some kind metrics. Now we try to use fuzzy logical formula based on distance function to define granular systems. There are three distance axioms: (1) $dis(A, A) = 0$; (2) $dis(A, B) = dis(B, A)$; (3) $dis(A, B) + dis(B, C) \geq dis(A, C)$. $dis(X, Y) < r$ defines a tolerance relation and $dis(X, Y) = 0$ defines an equivalent relation, and every tolerance relation can be viewed as an abstract distance which does not obey (d_3), so any granular systems based on equivalent relation and tolerance relation can be described by distance function in a geometrical way.

Definition 1 *[Simple fuzzy logical formula and intrinsic graph] A simple fuzzy logical formula based on distance function $sp(A, C|dis, d, W_\omega)$ is denoted as:*

$$sp(A, C|dis, d, W_\omega) = m(dis(A, C|W_\omega), d)) \tag{2.1}$$

where "$\circ$" is the dot product, $dis(A, C|W_\omega) = dis(A \circ W_\omega, C \circ W_\omega)$, $X \circ W_\omega = (x_1 w_{\omega_1}, ..., x_n w_{\omega_n})$, and $dis()$ is a point to point distance function, and W_ω is a weight vector for dimensions of a feature vector space $\mathbb{S}$, denoted as "dimensional weight'. $m()$ can be viewed as a membership function of a fuzzy set, it is usually a continuous function. For example

$$m(dis(A, C|W_\omega), d) = \begin{cases} (d - dis(A, C|W_\omega))/d, \ dis(A, C|W_\omega) < d \\ 0 \ , \ dis(A, C|W_\omega) \geq d \end{cases} \tag{2.2}$$

Please pay attention that simple fuzzy logical formulaes can create an intrinsic graph, which can be described by an

Page 14

intrinsic matrix. Every element of an intrinsic matrix is just a simple fuzzy logical formula. We define the r-cut set of $sp(A, C|dis, d, W_\omega)$ as:

$sp^r(A, C|dis, d, W_\omega) = sp(A, C|dis, d, W_\omega) > r$ *(strong r-cut set) or*
$\overline{sp^r}(A, C|dis, d, W_\omega) = sp(A, C|dis, d, W_\omega) \geq r$ *(r-cut set).*

$sp^r(X, C|dis, d, W_\omega)$ *defines an open convex region and denoted as a granule, and* $\overline{sp^r}(X, C|dis, d, W_\omega)$ *defines a closed convex region.*

Definition 2 *[A compound fuzzy logical proposition based on distance functions] A compound fuzzy logical proposition based on distance functions $P(A, B|\textbf{DIS}, D, \mathbb{C}, W_\omega)$ is a composite fuzzy logical function of a group $sp_i(A, C_i, -B|dis_i, d_i, W_\omega), i = 1, \cdots, k$, composed by "$\vee$" , "$\wedge$" and "$\rightarrow$" fuzzy logical operators, here $D = \{d_1, d_2, \cdots, d_k\}$ is a radius's set and $\mathbb{C} = \{C_1, C_2, \cdots, C_k\}$ is a centers'set, d_i and C_i are the radius and the center of $sp_i(A, C_i, -B|disi, d_i, W_\omega), (0 \leq i \leq k)$, respectively; and $\textbf{DIS} = \{dis_1, dis_2, \cdots, dis_k\}$ is a set of distance functions. For simplicity, the dimensional weight in all $sp_i(A, C_i, -B|dis_i, d_i, W_\omega)$ is same.*

Definition 3 *[Representing proposition of an arbitrary connected n-dimensional region $\mathbb{A}$ in R^n] If every point in a region $\mathbb{A}$ has a n-dimensional neighborhood which is included in $\mathbb{A}$, such kind region $\mathbb{A}$ is denoted as a n-dimensional region. Representing an arbitrary connected n-dimensional region $\mathbb{A}$ by a compound fuzzy logical proposition in a granulating process of region covering is defined as:*

if $\boldsymbol{S}_c$ is a set of granules' simple fuzzy logical formulas, and a compound fuzzy logical proposition $F(\boldsymbol{S}_c)$ is created from $\boldsymbol{S}_c$ by fuzzy logical operators "$\vee$" , "$\wedge$" and "$\rightarrow$" , then $F(\boldsymbol{S}_c)$ is denoted as a representation of $\mathbb{A}$ by S_c with error $1 > \varepsilon > 0$, if there is a $r \geq 0$, the volume difference between $|V(\mathbb{A} \cap S_n^r(F(\boldsymbol{S}_c))) - V(\mathbb{A} \cup S_n^r(F(\boldsymbol{S}_c)))| < \varepsilon$, where $V(\mathbb{X})$ is the volume of the region $\mathbb{X}$ and $S_n^r(F(\boldsymbol{S}_c))$ is the r- cut set of $F(\boldsymbol{S}_c)$. $1 - \varepsilon$ is denoted as the precision of $F(\boldsymbol{S}_c)$.

Theorem 1 promises that we can find a representation of $\mathbb{A}$ by Sc for arbitrary small error $1 > \varepsilon > 0$.

Theorem 1 *Every n-dimensional region $\mathbb{T}$ in $\mathbb{R}^n$ with finite volume can be described by a compound fuzzy logical proposition with arbitrary precision.*

Proof. Because $\mathbb{R}^n$ is tight, this theorem can be directly proved by the theorem of finite covering in mathematical analysis.$\square$

Definition 4 *[Leveled perception granular system based on tolerance relation Gsys] A granular system based on tolerance relations of distance functions (granular system for short and denoted as $\boldsymbol{Gsys}$) is a set of granules. Every granule $G(coeG^l)$ is a 2-tuple $\{\mathbb{G}_l, \boldsymbol{S}_{F_l}\}$, here $\mathbb{G}_l$ is a convex region which is described by tolerance relations of some distance functions, and $\boldsymbol{S}_{F_l}$ is a set of fuzzy logical functions (denoted as "adjoint functions") which are computed upon the convex region $\mathbb{G}_l$, the outputs of all fuzzy logical functions in $\boldsymbol{S}_{F_l}$ are denoted as "an adjoint feature vectors" of this granule. So $\boldsymbol{Gsys} = \{\mathbb{C}_{ov,l}, l = 1, \cdots, n_L\}$ can be formally described in the metric space $\mathbb{X}$*

(e.g. a finite connected n-dimensional region in the n-dimensional real space $\mathbb{R}^n$) as:

$$\{\mathbb{C}_{ov,l+1}, \mathbf{S}_{fea,l+1}\} = \{\mathbf{F}_g(C_{ov,l}), \mathbf{F}_{fea}(\mathbf{S}_{fea,l})\}. \tag{2.3}$$

here $\mathbb{C}_{ov,l} = \{\mathbb{G}_l\}$ is the set of all level l convex regions of granules which are hierarchically described by $\mathbf{F}_g$, and $\mathbf{F}_g$ is a compound fuzzy logical proposition based on distance function. $\mathbf{S}_{fea,l}$ is the set of all feature vectors of level l which are hierarchically computed by some fuzzy logical functions $\mathbf{F}_{fea}(\cdot)$.

The granules of $Gsys$ have the following attributions.

1. Multi-Scale Leveled Structure:

   We denote $\mathbb{S}^r_{setP}(l) = \{sp^r(X, C_i^{l+1}|dis^{l+1}, d_i^{l+1}, W_\omega) \mid i = 1, \cdots, k_{l+1}\}$ as the set of all r-cut subsets of simple fuzzy logical functions used in the level $l + 1$, here k_{l+1} is denoted as the number of simple fuzzy logical functions in the $l + 1th$-level. For the sake of simplicity, $sp^r(X, C_i^{l+1}|dis^{l+1}, d_i^{l+1}, W_\omega)$ is simplified as " sp_i^r ". Here the weight $W_\omega = (w_{\omega_1}, \cdots, w_{\omega_n})$, and $w_{\omega_j} \geq 0, j = 1, \cdots, n$. If $w_{\omega_j} > 0$, the corresponding dimension j of features' space is denoted as "**location dimension**".

   Level 0:

   The metric space X is the only level 0 granule, the level 0 granule is denoted as $G(coeG^0) = \{X, \mathbf{S}_{F_0}\}$, where $coeG^0$ is a coefficients' set, $coeG^0$ is usually empty, and the set $\mathbf{S}_{F_0}$ is a set of fuzzy logical functions (denoted as adjoint functions).

   Level 1:

   The convex region of a level 1 granule $G(coeG^1) = \{\mathbb{G}^1, \mathbf{S}_{F_1}\}$ is defined by the conjunction of finite number r-cut sets and the region X :

   $$\bigcap_{sp_i^r \in \mathbb{S}} sp^r(X, C_i^1|dis^1, d_i^1, W_\omega) \bigcap X,$$

   where $\mathbb{S} \subseteq \mathbb{S}^r_{setP}(1)$, $coeG^1 = \{coefficients \ of \ sp_i^r \in \mathbb{S}\}$ is its coefficients' set to define the convex region $\mathbb{G}^1$. For the sake of simplicity, $\mathbb{G}^1$ can also be written)as $G(coeG^1$

   Level $l + 1$:

   If the lth-level granules $G(coeG^l) = \{\mathbb{G}^l, \mathbf{S}_{F_l}\}$ have been defined, we define $\mathbb{S}^r_{G(coeG^l)} = \{sp_i^r \mid sp^r(A, C_i^{l+1}|dis^{l+1}, d_i^{l+1}, W_\omega) \bigcap G(coeG) \neq \emptyset, 1 \leq i \leq k_{l+1}\}$ as the subset of all simple fuzzy logical functions' r-subsets connected with $G(coeG^l)$. A $l + 1th$-level granule $G(coeG^{l+1})$, which is denoted as a son granule of $G(coeG^1)$, can be defined as :

   $$G(coeG^{l+1}) = \bigcap_{sp_i^r \in \mathbb{S} \subseteq \mathbb{S}_{G(coeG^l)}} sp^r(A, C_i^{l+1}|dis^{l+1}, d_i^{l+1}, W_\omega) \bigcap G(coeG^l),$$

   where a level $l + 1$ granule's coefficient is $coeG^{l+1} = \{C_i^{l+1}, d_i^{l+1}, dis^{l+1} \mid sp_i^r \in \mathbb{S}\}$, and $\mathbb{C}(G(coeG^{l+1})) = \{C_i^{l+1} \mid sp_i^r \in \mathbb{S}\}$ is the centers'set of $G(coeG^{l+1})$, and its radius d_i^{l+1} accords with $d_i^{l+1} \leq d_j^l$ for all $i = 1, \cdots, k_{l+1}$ and $j = 1, \cdots, k_l$, for more $\lim_{l \to \infty} d_i^l = 0$. The $G(coeG^l)$ is called as the "the father granule of $G(coeG^{l+1})$" and the "$l + 1th$-level cover of X is denoted as $\mathbb{C}^{l+1}_{ov}(X) = \{G(coeG^l)\}$.

2. Granular Deep Learning (GDL): A granular deep learning is described upon above multi scale leveled structure of convex regions for computing adjoint feature vectors.The purpose of a granular deep learning(GDL) is to transfer feature information and classify points in an input space X, so at least one level

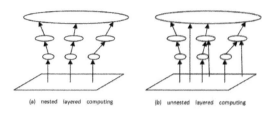

Figure 2.1: Two kind layered computing over granular system.

of a granular deep learning(GDL) outputs a fuzzy label for points in an input space $\mathbb{X}$. If there are totally m classes, a fuzzy label L is a m dimensional fuzzy vector $L = \{l_1, l_2., ..., l_m\}$, and $\sum_{i=1,...,m} l_i = 1$.

Just as above mentioned, adjoint feature vectors are outputs of a set of fuzzy logical functions $\boldsymbol{S_{F_l}}$.

JL Castro1995 [8] proved that Fuzzy logic controllers using fuzzy rules are universal approximations, later, Li H X .et al.(2000) [36] shows a proof of the equality between a forward neural circuit(or circuit) and a fuzzy logical inference. So it is not difficulty to prove that any continuous functions $F : \mathbb{R}^n \longrightarrow [0,1]^n$ can be simulated by such kind nested layered granular deep learning with arbitrary small errors. Based on these facts, for the sake of simplicity, in some layers, some functions in $\boldsymbol{S_{F_l}}$ can be arranged as usual continuous functions, i.e. the definition of GDL can be modified as:

Granular deep learning is completed by a set of layered functions denoted as " **adjoint functions**", and the vectors computed by GDL is denoted as "**adjoint feature vectors**".

The level of a GDL is upside down with the level of the $Gsys$. If a leveled granular system Gsys has k levels, GDL is taken from level k to 1. The 1st level GDL takes place in the smallest kth level granules'convex regions of $Gsys$. A level $l + 1$ adjoint function F_{l+1} receives its input from the outputs of level p adjoint functions , $1 \leq p \leq l$, and outputs a level $l + 1$ adjoint feature vector.

Two kinds layered computing can be taken place over a granular system. In the first kind layered computing, the adjoint feature vectors of larger scale granules(level n) are computed based on the adjoint feature vectors of smaller scale granules(level $n + 1$), such kind layered computing has strictly nested structure,(Fig. 2.1(a)), and is denoted as "nested layered computing". In the second kind layered computing, adjoint feature vectors of level n granules can be computed based on all adjoint feature vectors of smaller granules, which have levels greater than n (Fig. 2.1(b)), such kind layered computing is denoted as "unnested layered computing". Nested layered computing is a special case of unnested layered computing.

3. **Radiuses of Convex Regions:** A granular system can have countable infinite or finite levels. The radiuses of granules'convex regions decrease and tend to zero when the level goes to infinite.

4. **Centers' Grid:** The centers of granules will distribute in a so called center grid. We denote the set of all centers of level $l + 1$ granules on the granule $G(coeG^l)$ as Gc^{l+1} $(G(coeG^l))$. We denote the set of all centers of level $l + 1$ granules over X as $Gc^{l+1}(X)$ and all centers of level $l + 1$ granules over a level $k < l$ granule

$G(coeG^k)$ as $Gc^{l+1}(G(coeG^k))$.

The center grid is usually discrete, but it can also be a continuous set e.g. the whole metric space X.

5. **Shape of Granules:** all granules are convex regions, which are determined by the shapes of the r-cut sets $sp^r(A, C_i^{l+1}|dis^{l+1}, d_i^{l+1}, W_\omega)$ and their father granules'shapes. The shape of a r-cut set is determined by its distance function $dis()$. If $dis()$ can be an abstract distance function, then a r-cut set can be an arbitrary convex region.

6. **Cover Over a Granule:** In order to create a cover over $G(coeG^l)$,the centers' grid Gc^{l+1} $(G(coeG^l))$ should be tight enough. Such kind cover can be formerly defined as:

$$C_{ov}^{l+1}(G(coeG^l))$$
$$= \{G(coeG^{l+1}) \mid G(coeG^{l+1}) \bigcap G(coeG^l) \neq \phi\}$$

All level $l+1$ granules create a cover of the whole space $\mathbb{X}$, and denoted as the level $l+1$ cover or the level $l+1$ layer of $\mathbb{X}$, $C_{ov}^{l+1}(\mathbb{X}) = \underset{G(coeG^l) \in C_{ov}^l(\mathbb{X})}{\cup} \{C_{ov}^{l+1}(G(coeG^l))\}$.

Radial Basis neural network [23], which can be used to simulate continuous functions, is an example of two layers granule system. In fact, feedback can be introduced in a layered granular system, we define the granular computing with feedback as "Recurrent Granular Computing".

Definition 5 *[Recurrent Granular Computing] In the definition 4, if a level $l+1$ adjoint function F_{l+1} can receive its input from the outputs of level $l + p, p \leq 0$ adjoint functions, i.e. some feedbacks can be used in the GrC, such kind granular computing is denoted as recurrent granular computing.*

In a granular system, if all relations of granules can be described by fuzzy logic, such kind leveled perception granular system is denoted as " *leveled fuzzy granular system*", in this case, granular computing can be represented as a fuzzy logical formula.

Definition 6 *[Hyper-granules and mini-granules] All level $n+1$ granules $G(coeG^{n+1})$, which are contained in a level n granule $G(coeG^n)$, are denoted as "mini-granules" of $G(coeG^n)$, and the corresponding level n granule $G(coeG^n)$ is denoted as a "hyper-granule".*

Chapter 3

Hybrid Designing of Leveled Perception Granular System

In order to design a granular system for simulating the perception cognition of our brain, a suitable fuzzy logical operator should be selected at first, such kind fuzzy operator should be easy for designing a $Gsys$ and can be simulated by a neural cell.

At other hand, Sigmoid function whos graph is s-shaped, is by far the most common form of activation function used in the construction of artificial neural system. Can we use Sigmoid function in a granular computing? the answer is "yes", in this chapter, we also prove that if the logistic function is used as a Sigmoid function, it can simulate fuzzy logical operator perfectly, so Sigmoid function can be used in the layered computing of a Granular system based on tolerance relation.

3.1 q-Value Weighted Bounded Operator

After the theory of fuzzy logic was conceived by Zadeh [69], many fuzzy logical systems have been presented, for example, the Zadeh system, the probability system, the algebraic system, and Bounded operator system, etc. We should select a suitable fuzzy operator for granular computing. In this book, the extended Bounded operator is selected, which is denoted as "q-value Weighted Bounded operator". q-value Weighted Bounded operator can be approximately simulated by a neural cell with a Sigmoid function. According to universal approximation theorem [24], it is not difficult to prove that q-value weighted fuzzy logical formulas can precisely simulate any continuous functions $F : [0,1]^n \longrightarrow [0,1]$ with arbitrary small error, or vice versa, i.e. **every GrC can be completed by a set of fuzzy logical functions of q-value weighted bounded operator with arbitrary small error.**

Definition 7 *[Bounded Operator $F(\oplus_f, \otimes_f)$] Bounded product: $x \otimes_f y = \max(0, x + y - 1)$, and Bounded sum: $x \oplus_f y = \min(1, x + y)$, where $0 \leq x, y \leq 1$.*

In order to simulate granular computing, it is necessary to extend the Bounded Operator to Weighted Bounded Operator. The fuzzy formulas defined by q-value weighted bounded operators is denoted as q-value weighted fuzzy logical functions.

Definition 8 *[q-value Weighted Bounded operator $F(\oplus_f, \otimes_f)$] q-value Weighted Bounded product:*

$$
\begin{aligned}
p_1 \otimes_f p_2 &= F_{\otimes_f}(p_1, p_2, w_1, w_2) \\
&= \max(0, w_1 p_1 + w_2 p_2 - (w_1 + w_2 - 1)q)
\end{aligned} \tag{3.1}
$$

q-value Weighted Bounded sum:

$$
p_1 \oplus_f p_2 = F_{\oplus_f}(p_1, q_2, w_1, w_2) = \min(q, w_1 p_1 + w_2 p_2) \tag{3.2}
$$

where $0 \le p_1, p_2 \le q$.

For association and distribution rules, we define:

$(p_1 \Delta_f p_2) \Theta_f p_3 = F_{\Theta_f}(F_{\Delta_f}(p_1, p_2, w_1, w_2), p_3, 1, w_3)$ and $p_1 \Delta_f(p_2 \Theta_f p_3) = F_{\Delta_f}(p_1, F_{\Theta_f}(p_2, p_3, w_2, w_3), w_1, 1)$,

Here $\Delta_f, \Theta_f = \otimes_f \mathrm{or} \oplus_f$. We can prove that $\oplus_f$ and $\otimes_f$ follow the associative condition(see Appendix) and

$$
x_1 \oplus_f x_2 \oplus_f x_3 ... \oplus_f x_n = \min(q, \sum_{1 \le i \le n} w_i x_i) \tag{3.3}
$$

$$
\begin{aligned}
&x_1 \otimes_f x_2 \otimes_f x_3 ... \otimes_f x_n \\
&= \max(0, \sum_{1 \le i \le n} w_i x_i - (\sum_{1 \le i \le n} w_i - 1)q)
\end{aligned} \tag{3.4}
$$

For more above q-value weighted bounded operator $F(\oplus_f, \otimes_f)$ follows the Demorgan Law, i.e.

$$
\begin{aligned}
N(x_1 \oplus_f x_2 \oplus_f x_3 ... \oplus_f x_n) &= q - \min(q, \sum_{1 \le i \le n} w_i x_i) \\
&- \max(0, q - \sum_{1 \le i \le n} w_i x_i) \\
&= \max(0, \sum_{1 \le i \le n} w_i (q - x_i) - (\sum_{1 \le i \le n} w_i - 1)q) \\
&= N(x_1) \otimes_f N(x_2) \otimes_f N(x_3) ... \otimes_f N(x_n).
\end{aligned} \tag{3.5}
$$

But for the q-value weighted bounded operator $F(\oplus_f, \otimes_f)$, the distribution condition is usually not hold, and the boundary condition is hold only all weights equal to 1, for $p_1 \otimes_f q = F_{\otimes_f}(p_1, q, w_1, w_2) = \max(0, w_1 p_1 + (1 - w_1)q)$ and $p_1 \oplus_f q = F_{\oplus_f}(p_1, q, w_1, w_2) = \min(q, w_1 p_1 + w_2 q)$.

3.2 Sigmoid function and Logic

Just as above mentioned, the sigmoid function whos graph is s-shaped, is by far the most common form of activation function used in the construction of artificial neural system. Now It is defined as a strictly increasing function that exhibits a graceful balance between linear and nonlinear behavior(Simon Haykin, 1999). In the following pages, we try to show that a computing which combines sigmoid function and linear function can simulate binary logical operator or a q-value weighted fuzzy logical operator, this fact means that layered neural networks can be used to design above mentioned granular system.

Sigmoid function can be identified as three basic types:

1. Logistic function :

$$S(u_i - t_i) = \frac{1}{1 + \exp(-\lambda(u_i - t_i))}$$

Where λ is the slope parameter of the sigmoid function.

2. Piecewise-Linear function:

$$S(u_i - t_i) = \begin{cases} 1, & u_i - t_i > 1 \\ u_i - t_i, & 1 \geq u_i - t_i \geq 0 \\ 0, & u_i - t_i < 0 \end{cases}$$

3. Hyperbolic tangent function:

$$S(u_i - t_i) = \tanh(u_i - t_i)$$

In this book, if not point out, the logistic function is used as the sigmoid function. Eq. (3.6) which is the statical point of a dynamical Hopfield neuron (EQ. (4.1)) is an example of using the logistic function, the theorem 2 probes the relation between the logistic function and binary logic.

$$\bar{v}_n = \frac{1}{[\exp(-\lambda(\bar{u}_n - t_n) + 1)]} \tag{3.6}$$

here $\bar{u}_n = \frac{\sum\limits_{1 \leq k \leq K} w_{n,k} x_k}{a_n}$.

Theorem 2 *Suppose in Eq. (3.6), every $a_n = 1$, $w_{n,k} = \beta_k t_n, \beta_k > 0, t_n > 0, 1 \leq k \leq K$, for more, $C = \{S_i | i = 1, ..., L\}$ is a class of index sets, and every index set S_i is a subset of $\{1, 2, 3, ..., K\}$, then we have :*

1. *If $f(x_1, x_2, ..., x_k) = \bigvee\limits_{l=1,...,L} (\bigwedge\limits_{j_i \in S_i} x_{j_i})$ is a disjunctive normal form (DNF) formula, and the class $C = \{S_i | i = 1, ..., L\}$ is the class which has the following two characters:*

   (1). for every $S_i, S_j \in C, S_i \cap S_j \neq S_k \in C$ for all k and $i \neq j$(this condition assures that $f(x_1, x_2, ..., x_k)$ has a simplest form);

   (2). every S_i has the character $\sum\limits_{j \in S_i} \beta_j > 1$, where $S_i \in C$, and any index sets $S' \notin C$ have character $\sum\limits_{j \in S'} \beta_j < 1$, or if $\sum\limits_{j \in S'} \beta_j > 1$, there must be an index set $S_i \in C$ such that $S' \cap S_i = S_i$(this condition assures C is the largest), then the output described by Eq. (3.6) can simulate the DNF formula $f(x_1, x_2, ..., x_k) = \bigvee\limits_{l=1,...,L} (\bigwedge\limits_{i \in S_i} x_{j_i})$ with arbitrary small error, where $x_i = z_i$ or $x_i = \bar{z}_i$, if the corresponding input for Eq. (3.6) is $x_i = z_i$ or $x_i = 1 - z_i$ respectively.

2. *If a neural cell described by Eq. (3.6) can simulate the Boolean formula $f(x_1, x_2, ..., x_k)$ with arbitrary small error, and $(\bigwedge\limits_{i \in S_l} x_i)$ is an item in the disjunctive normal form of $f(x_1, x_2, ..., x_k)$, i.e. $f(x_1, x_2, ..., x_k) = 1$ at $x_j = 1$ for all $j \in S_l$ and $x_j = 0$ for all $j \notin S_l$, then $\sum\limits_{i \in S_l} \beta_i > 1$.*

3. *If a couple of index sets S_{l_1} and S_{l_2} can be found in the formula $f(x_1, x_2, ..., x_k) = \bigvee\limits_{l=1,...,k} (\bigwedge\limits_{t \in S_l} x_t)$, such that $(\bigwedge\limits_{t_1 \in S_{l_1}} x_{t_1}) \wedge (\bigwedge\limits_{t_2 \in S_{l_2}} x_{t_2}) = z_i \wedge \bar{z}_i = false$, then the output described by Eq. (3.6) can't simulate the formula $f(x_1, x_2, ..., x_k)$.*

Proof:

1. If $x_t = 1$, for all $t \in S_l$, and $x_t = 0$, for all $t \notin S_l$, because $\sum_{i \in S_l} \beta_i > 1$, then for the index set S_l is a subset of $\{1, 2, 3, \ldots, K\}$, we have

$$\bar{v}_n = 1/[\exp(-\lambda(\bar{u}_n - t_n) + 1]$$
$$= 1/[\exp(-\lambda(\sum_{1 \leq k \leq K} w_{n,k} x_k - t_n)) + 1] \quad,$$
$$= 1/[\exp(-\lambda(\sum_{i \in S_l} \beta_i - 1) t_n)) + 1]$$

so $\lim_{\lambda \to +\infty} \bar{v}_n = 1 = f(x_1, x_2, \ldots, x_K)$. If $x_t = 1, \forall t \in S'$; $x_t = 0, \forall t \notin S'$ and $S' \notin C$, then according to the condition of this theorem: if $\sum_{i \in S'} \beta_i < 1$, $\lim_{\lambda \to +\infty} \bar{v}_n = 0 = f(x_1, x_2, \ldots, x_K)$; if $\sum_{i \in S'} \beta_i > 1$, then there is an index set $S_i \in C$ such that $S' \cap S_i = S_i$, then $\lim_{\lambda \to +\infty} \bar{v}_n = 1 = f(x_1, x_2, \ldots, x_K)$. So when $\lambda \to \infty$, the error between output described by Eq. (3.6) and $f(x_1, x_2, \ldots, x_k)$ trends to 0.

2. For a definite binary input $x_1, x_2, \ldots, x_k$, if the output described by Eq. (3.6) can simulate the Boolean formula $f(x_1, x_2, \ldots, x_k)$ which is not a constant with arbitrary small error, then the arbitrary small error is achieved when λ trends to infinite and $(\bar{u}_n - t_n) = \sum_{k \in S_l} w_{n,k} x_k - t_n \neq 0$ where S_l is the set of the labels and $x_i = 1$, for all $i \in S_l$, and $x_i = 0$, for all $i \notin S_l$.

   The theorem's condition supposes that every $w_{n,k} = \beta_k t_n, \beta_k > 0, t_n > 0, 1 \leq k \leq K$, and $x_1, x_2, \ldots, x_K$ are binary number 0 or 1, so if $f(x_1, x_2, \ldots, x_K)$ is not a constant, when $f(x_1, x_2, \ldots, x_K) = 0$, there must be $\lim_{\lambda \to +\infty} \bar{v}_n = 0$; and when $f(x_1, x_2, \ldots, x_K) = 1$, it is necessary for $\lim_{\lambda \to +\infty} \bar{v}_n = 1$. $\lim_{\lambda \to +\infty} \bar{v}_n = 0$ needs that $-\lambda(\sum_{i \in S_l} \beta_i t_n - t_n)$ trends to minus infinite and $\lim_{\lambda \to +\infty} \bar{v}_n = 1$ needs that $-\lambda(\sum_{i \in S_l} \beta_i t_n - t_n)$ trends to plus infinite.

   So if $f(x_1, x_2, \ldots, x_K) = 1$ at $x_j = 1$ for all $j \in S_l$ and $x_j = 0$ for all, in order to guarantee $\lim_{\lambda \to +\infty} err_{f(x_1, x_2, \ldots, x_K)}(w_{n,1}, w_{n,2}, \ldots, w_{n,K}, t_n) = 0$, $\sum_{i \in S_l} \beta_i > 1$ must be hold, here $err_{f(x_1, x_2, \ldots, x_K)}(w_{i,1}, w_{i,2}, \ldots, w_{i,K}, t_i) = |\bar{v}_i - f(x_1, x_2, \ldots, x_K)|$ is the error between output described by Eq. (3.6) and $f(x_1, x_2, \ldots, x_K)$.

3. The third part of the theorem is based on the simple fact that the single neuron v_i is monotone on every input x_i in Eq. (3.6) , here x_i can be z_i or $1 - z_i$. $\square$

An example of the 3rd part of above theorem is the *xor* function which can't be simulated by the neuron described by Eq. (3.6).

If there are only two inputs $x_1, x_2(x_1, x_2 \in [0, 1])$ in Eq. (3.6), we set $w_1 = 1.0$ and $w_2 = 1.0$, then $\bar{u}_n = x_1 + x_2$. Now we try to prove that the Bounded operator $F(\oplus_f, \otimes_f)$ is the best fuzzy operator to simulate neural cells described by Eq. (3.6) and the threshold t_n can change the neural cell from the bounded operator $\oplus_f$ to $\otimes_f$. This fact can be showed in following two cases:

1. If $c > 0$ is a constant and $\bar{u}_n = x_1 + x_2 \geq c$, $1/(\exp(-c + t_n) + 1) \leq \bar{v}_n < 1$. In this case:
   (a). if $\bar{u}_n = x_1 + x_2 \to +\infty$, we have $\bar{v}_n \to 1$;
   (b). If c is large enough, we have $\bar{v}_n \approx 1$;
   (c). If $-c \leq \bar{u}_n = x_1 + x_2 \leq c$, then $1/(\exp(c + t_n) + 1) \leq \bar{v}_n \leq 1/(\exp(-c + t_n) + 1)$, according to Eq. (3.7). We can

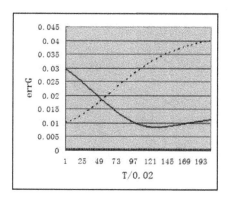

Figure 3.1: Simulating fuzzy logical and-or by changing thresholds of Eq. (3.6). The X-axis is the threshold value t divided by 0.02, the Y-axis is errG. The real line is errAnd between $x_1 \otimes_f x_2$ and $\bar{v}_n$, and the dot line is the errOr between $x_1 \oplus_f x_2$ and $\bar{v}_n$

select a t_n, that makes $|t_n + \sum_{j=2}^{\infty} (-\bar{u}_n + t_n)^j / j! - \sum_{k=2}^{\infty} (-1)^k \exp(-k(\bar{u}_n - t_n))|$ small enough, then $\bar{v}_n \approx x_1 + x_2$.

$$\bar{v}_n = \frac{1}{\exp(-\bar{u}_n + t_n) + 1)} = 1 - \exp(-\bar{u}_n + t_n) + \sum_{k=2}^{\infty} (-1)^k \exp(-k(\bar{u}_n - t_n))$$

$$= \bar{u}_n - t_n - \sum_{j=2}^{\infty} (-\bar{u}_n + t_n)^j / j! + \sum_{k=2}^{\infty} (-1)^k \exp(-k(\bar{u}_n - t_n)) \qquad (3.7)$$

$$= \bar{u}_n - t_n - \sum_{j=2}^{\infty} (-\bar{u}_n + t_n)^j / j! + \sum_{k=2}^{\infty} (-1)^k \exp(-k(\bar{u}_n - t_n))$$

So in this case, $\bar{v}_n \approx x_1 \oplus_f x_2 = \min(1, x_1 + x_2)$.

2. Similarly, if $\bar{u}_n = x_1 + x_2 \to -\infty$, $\bar{v}_n \to 0$. So when c is large enough and $\bar{u}_n = x_1 + x_2 \leq -c < 0$, then $\bar{v}_n \approx 0$. In this case, when $-c \leq \bar{u}_n = x_1 + x_2 \leq c$, if we select a suitable t_n which makes $t_n + \sum_{j=2}^{\infty} (-\bar{u}_n + t_n)^j / j! - \sum_{k=2}^{\infty} (-1)^k \exp(-k(\bar{u}_n - t_n)) \approx 1$, then $\bar{v}_n \approx x_1 \otimes_f x_2 = \max(0, x_1 + x_2 - 1)$.

The following experiment is done by scanning the whole region of (x_1, x_2) in $[0, 1]^2$ to find the suitable coefficients for $\oplus_f$ and $\otimes_f$ show that above analysis is sound. We denote the input in Eq. (3.6) as $X(t) = (x_1(t), x_2(t))$. Not loosing generality, the parameters are fixed as $a = 1.0$, $w_1 = 1.0$ and $w_2 = 1.0$. The "errAnd" for $\oplus_f$ and "errOr" for $\otimes_f$ are shown in Fig. 3.1 as the solid line and the dotted line respectively. In Fig.3.1, the threshold t_n is scanned from 0 to 4.1 with step size 0.01.

The best t_n in Eq. (3.6) for $\otimes_f$ is 2.54 and the best t_n in Eq. (3.6) for $\oplus_f$ is 0. In this case the "errOr" and "errAnd" is less than 0.01. Our experiments show that suitable t_n can be found. So in most cases, the bounded operator $F(\oplus_f, \otimes_f)$ mentioned above is the suitable leveled fuzzy granular system for the neuron defined by Eq. (3.6). If the weight $0 < w_1$ and $0 < w_2$, we can use a q-value weighted bounded operator $F(\oplus_f, \otimes_f)$ to simulate Eq. (3.6). Based on above analysis, for arbitrary positive a_n, w_1 and w_2, we can use corresponding q-value weighted universal

Page 23

fuzzy logical function based on Bounded operator to simulate it. So the Bounded operator fuzzy system is suitable for GDC described by Eq. (3.6). For a N-norm operator $N(x) = 1 - x$, the corresponding weight w should be negative.

3.3   Hybrid Designing of Leveled Perception Granular System Based on Fuzzy Logic, Back Propagation and PSVM

A nested layered GrC is defined by the input and output relation of a granular computing on a granular system. There are three kinds relations between nearby layers (layers k and $k+1$) of a nested GrC: (1) binary logic; (2)fuzzy logic; (3) alogical relation.

Because fuzzy logic and binary logic are all created by the sigmoid function, so back propagation method can be used to modify weights of all layers. In order to speed up the learning process, for a layered GrC, we combine logical designing with PSVM [18], such kind novel approach is called as "Logical support vector machine (LPSVM)". For a nested layered GrC, parameters in the binary logical layers can be directly designated according to the binary relation; for the fuzzy logical layers, parameters can also be set according to these layers'functions, but a suitable small adjustment by back propagation is necessary, this is similar to the deep learning proposed by Geoffrey Hinton [27] such that a many-layered neural network could be effectively pre-trained one layer at a time, treating each layer in turn as an unsupervised restricted Boltzmann machine,then using supervised backpropagation for fine-tuning. For the non logical (alogical) layer, parameters should be learned based on samples according to the input and output relation function $f_i(x_1, x_2, x_3, \ldots, x_n)$, we can use Back Propagation method or PSVM, to learn weights for $f_i(x_1, x_2, x_3, \ldots, x_n)$.

The designing strategy of LPSVM:

- Step 1: Except for the alogical layer's weights, designing the layers' weights according to the logical (binary or fuzzy) relations, for fuzzy logical relations, a suitable modification of weights maybe be necessary according to the task of this layer;

- Step 2: Alogical layers' weights are computed according to the relation of its input and output. For an alogical layer l, if $\mathbb{X}$ is the input train set of whole GDL, this layer's input $\mathbb{X}_l$ is computed from the 1st layer to the $(l-1)^{th}$ layer based on $\mathbb{X}$, then using PSVM to compute the lth layer's weights' vector W_l according to (3.8);

- Step 3: after the weights' vector W_l has been computed, using back propagating approach to modify all layers weights.

When previous layers' weights are computed based on the target, these previous layers' weights can also be modified by the least square method(see Appendix).

Page 24

- Step 4: Repeat the Step 2 to Step 3, until the output error is small enough.

$$W_l = \mathbb{X}_l{}' \mathbb{D} U \tag{3.8}$$

Where U is computed by (3.9) and $\mathbb{X}_l$ and $\mathbb{D}$ are the problem data, i.e. $\mathbb{X}_l = [X_{l,1}, ..., X_{l,n}]$, and diagonal

matrix $\mathbb{D} = \begin{bmatrix} y_1 & 0 & 0 \\ \vdots & \ddots & \vdots \\ 0 & \cdots & y_n \end{bmatrix}$, $(X_{l,j}, y_j)$ is a training sample with the feature vector $X_{l,j}$ and the target y_j.

$$U = \left(\frac{\mathbb{I}}{\nu} + \mathbb{D}(\mathbb{X}_l \mathbb{X}_l' + E \cdot E')\mathbb{D} \right)^{-1} E \tag{3.9}$$

Where ν is a positive parameter selected for guarantee of a small magnitude $\|W_l\|$, $\mathbb{I}$ is the identity matrix, and E is a vector with all elements are 1.

Chapter 4

Granular Computing in the Static State of a Layered Dynamical Neural System

A layered dynamical neural network usually converges to a steady or static state. Hopfield neural network(Eq. (4.1)) uses logistic function as its output function, so its steady state described by Eq. (3.6) has very sound logical character (see Theorem 2), so above mentioned fuzzy granular computing can be completed in a layered Hopfield neural network. For more, in this chapter, we prove that Hopfield neural networks can simulate a lot of neuron models with arbitrary small error, so a granular computing can also be completed in the steady or static state of most layered neural networks.

4.1 Hopfield model

There are many neuron models, e.g. Fitz Hugh ,(1961), Morris, Lecar (1981), Chay (1985) and Hindmarsh, Rose (1984), [16,26,60]. Whether the fuzzy logical approach can be used in all kinds of neural networks for different neuron models? In order to answer this question, we consider a simple neuron model- Hopfield model (see Eq. (4.1)) [31] as a standard neuron model, which has a good character of fuzzy logic. We have proved that Hopfield model has universal meaning, such that almost all neural models described by first order differential equations can be simulated by them with arbitrary small error in an arbitrary finite time interval [32], these neural models include all the models summarized by H D I [65].

$$\dot{u}_i = -a_i \cdot u_i + \sum_j w'_{ij} v_j + \beta \sum_k w_{ik} x_k;$$
$$v_i = S(u_i - t_i)$$

$$(4.1)$$

where sigmoid function $S()$ can be a piecewise linear function or logistic function, a_i is a time coefficient, which controls the running speed of a neuron, w'_{ij} and w_{ij} are connected weights and input weights respectively. Hopfield neuron model has a notable biological characteristic and has been widely used in visual cortex simulation. One example of them is described in [17,56,60]), (see Eq. (4.2)). Such cellos membrane potential is transferred to output by a sigmoid-like function. Only the amplitude of output pluses carries meaningful information. The rising or dropping time (Δt) of output pluses conveys no useful information and is always neglected. According to [39, 75], the neural networks described by Eq. (4.2) are based on biological data [2, 4, 20, 33, 54, 59].

In such kind neural networks, cells are arranged on a regular 2-dimensional array with image coordinates $i = (n_i, m_i)$ and divided into two categories: excitatory cells $x_{i\theta}$ and inhibitory cells $y_{i\theta}$. At every position $i = (n_i, m_i)$, there are m cells with subscript t_θ that are sensitive to a bar of the angle θ. Eq. (4.2) is the dynamical equation of these cells. Only excitatory cells receive inputs from the outputs of edge or bar detectors. The direction information of edges or bars is used for segmentation of the optical image.

$$
\begin{aligned}
\dot{x}_{i\theta} &= -a_x x_{i\theta} - g_y(y_{i\theta}) + J_c g_x(x_{i\theta}) + x_c - \\
&\quad \sum_{\nabla\theta\neq0} \psi(\nabla\theta) g_y(y_{i,\theta+\nabla\theta}) + \sum_{j\neq i,\theta'} J_{i\theta,j\theta'} g_x(x_{j\theta'}) + x_{i\theta}; \\
\dot{y}_{i\theta} &= -a_y y_{i\theta} - g_x(x_{i\theta}) + g_x(x_{i\theta}) + x_c + \\
&\quad \sum_{j\neq i,\theta'} W_{i\theta,j\theta'} g_x(x_{j\theta'}).
\end{aligned}
\tag{4.2}
$$

where $g_x(x)$ and $g_y(x)$ are sigmoid-like activation functions, and ψ is the local inhibition connection in the location i, and $J_{i\theta,j\theta'}$ and $W_{i\theta,j\theta'}$ are the synaptic connections between the excitatory cells and from the excitatory cells to inhibition cells, respectively. If we represent the excitatory cells and inhibitory cells with same symbol u_i and summarize all connections (local ψ, global exciting $W_{i\theta,j\theta'}$ and global inhibiting $J_{i\theta,j\theta'}$) as w'_{ij}, the Eq. (4.2) can be simplified as Hopfield model Eq. (4.1).

4.2 Leveled Fuzzy Logical Framework in a Layered Dynamical Neural Network

In order to design a dynamical neural network based on the theory of our granular computing, we should probe the relationship between the structures of a fuzzy logical formula and a layered dynamical neural network. As Same fuzzy logical function can have several equivalent formats; these formats can be viewed as the structure of a fuzzy function. When we discuss the relationship between the fuzzy logic and neural network, we should not only probe the input-output relationship but also their corresponding structure.

4.2.1 Structure of a fuzzy logical function and a neural network

A recurrent dynamical neural network can be designed by combining several layered neural networks, Theorem 4 gives out an example of how to simulate a recurrent neural network by several layered neural networks. So if the relation of the structures between layered neural networks and leveled fuzzy logical functions has been clearly understood, to design a recurrent dynamical neural network may become an easy task. For this purpose, in this chapter, we try to define several concepts which can be used to probe the relation of layered fuzzy logical functions and layered neural networks. Of cause these concepts can also be augmented to recurrent fuzzy logical function and neural networks. In order to easily map a leveled fuzzy granular system to a dynamical neural network, we should define the concept about the structure of a fuzzy logical function.

Definition 9 *[The structure of a leveled fuzzy logical function] If S^1 is a set of fuzzy logical functions(FLF), and a FLF $f(x_1, x_2, \ldots, x_n)$ can be represented by the combination of all FLFs in S^1 with fuzzy operators "$\wedge$", "$\vee$" and "$\neg$", but with no parentheses, then the FLFs in S^1 is denoted as the 1st layer sub fuzzy logical functions (1st FLF) of $f(x_1, x_2, \ldots, x_n)$; similarly, if a variable x_i in a FLF in S^1 is an output of a function, i.e. $x_i = f_1(y_1, y_2, \ldots, y_n)$, then $f_1(y_1, y_2, \ldots, y_n)$ has its own 1st layer sub FLFs which are denoted as the 2nd layer sub FLFs of $f(x_1, x_2, \ldots, x_n) \ldots$, and every k^{th} layer non variable sub FLF can have its sub fuzzy logical functions. In this way, $f(x_1, x_2, \ldots, x_n)$ has a layered structure of sub fuzzy logical functions, we denote such layered structure as the structure of $f(x_1, x_2, \ldots, x_n)$.*

For example, $f(x_1, x_2, x_3, x_4)$ in Fig. 4.1 can be represented by $f_1(x_1, x_2) = x_1 \wedge x_2$ and $f_2(x_2, x_3, x_4) = x_2 \wedge x_3 \vee x_4$ as $f_1(x_1, x_2) \vee f_2(x_2, x_3, x_4)$, so $f_1(x_1, x_2)$ and $f_2(x_2, x_3, x_4)$ are the 1st layer $FLFs$ in S^1.

$f(x_1, x_2, \ldots, x_n)$ may have several equivalent formats, so the structure of $f(x_1, x_2, \ldots, x_n)$ is not unique, for example, $f(x_1, x_2, x_3, x_4) = x_1 \wedge x_2 \vee x_2 \wedge x_3 \vee x_4 = x_1 \wedge x_2 \vee (x_2 \wedge x_3 \vee x_4) = ((x_1 \wedge x_2) \vee (x_2 \wedge x_3)) \vee x_4 \ldots$, can be represented as trees (a) and (b) in Fig. 4.1. If a sub fuzzy logical function is just $f(x_1, x_2, \ldots, x_n)$ itself, then $f(x_1, x_2, \ldots, x_n)$ has a recurrent structure, otherwise, $f(x_1, x_2, \ldots, x_n)$ has a tree kind structure.

The definition 10 is the measure about the difference between a leveled fuzzy logical function and a layered neural network.

Definition 10 *[Difference error between a leveled fuzzy logical function and a layered neural network] A layered neural network must have a static or fixed point. If $X(t)$ is an input, and the region of input $X(t)$ is $\mathbb{D}$. The difference error between a leveled fuzzy logical function G and a layered neural network F is defined as:*
Static case:

$$err_G = \sum_{X \in D} |G(X) - F(X)|,$$
$$\text{where } F(X) \text{ is the fixed point of } F \tag{4.3}$$

Above definition can be augmented to the recurrent case. If $f(x_1, x_2, \ldots, x_n)$ has a recurrent structure, then it can be represented as Eq. (4.4). For more if we suppose that the delay time needed for its output is Δt and $f^t(x_1, x_2, \ldots, x_n)$ is linearly changed to $f^{t+\Delta t}(x_1, x_2, \ldots, x_n)$, then $f(x_1, x_2, \ldots, x_n)$ can create a time serial output and can be written in partial differential form as Eq. (4.5).

$$f(x_1, x_2, \ldots, x_n) = g(x_1, x_2, \ldots, x_n, f(x_1, x_2, \ldots, x_n)) \tag{4.4}$$

$$f^{(t+dt)}(x_1, x_2, \ldots, x_n) = f^t(x_1, x_2, \ldots, x_n)$$
$$+[g(f^t(x_1, x_2, \ldots, x_n), x_1, x_2, \ldots, x_n)$$
$$-f^t(x_1, x_2, \ldots, x_n)]dt/\Delta t \tag{4.5}$$

Where $(x_1, x_2, \ldots, x_n)$ is a stable input vector which can be viewed as an initial condition of a dynamical system and $0 \leq dt \leq \Delta t$. The difference error between a recurrent fuzzy logical function and a recurrent neural network can be defined as:

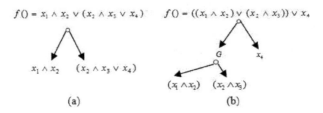

Figure 4.1: $f(x_1, x_2, ..., x_n)$ may have several equivalent formats, so the structure of $f(x_1, x_2, ..., x_n)$ is not unique.

Definition 11 *[Difference error between a recurrent fuzzy logical function and a recurrent neural network]*

$$err_G = \int_0^T |G(X(t)) - F(X(t))|dt \tag{4.6}$$

where the input domain for $X(t)$ is $\mathbb{D}$, the dynamical behavior of a neural network can be described as $Y(t) = F(X(t))$, $G(X(t))$ is a FLF with same dynamical variables in $X(t)$, and $Y_G(t) = G(X(t))$ is the dynamical behavior of a fuzzy logical function, here $X(t)$ and $Y_G(t)$ are input and output at t respectively.

Usually, a neural model can only approximately simulate a fuzzy operator, so it is necessary to find the most similar fuzzy function for a leveled neural network, which is denoted as the leveled fuzzy granular system of a neural network, the definition 12 gives out the concept of the fuzzy logical framework.

Definition 12 *[The leveled fuzzy granular system of a neural network] Suppose Ω is a set of fuzzy logical functions, a leveled fuzzy granular system for a layered neural network F is the best fuzzy logical function G in Ω satisfied the constrain that G has smallest err_G i.e. $err_G = \min_{G' \in \Omega} err_{G'}$. If there is a one to one onto mapping from neurons in a layered neural network F to the all layers sub fuzzy logical functions in a G's structure, such kind leveled fuzzy granular system is denoted as structure keeping leveled fuzzy granular system.*

Just above mentioned according to universal approximation theorem [24], it is not difficult to prove that q-value weighted fuzzy logical functions(Definition 8) can precisely simulate some layered neural networks, e.g. Hopfield neural networks(Eq (4.1)), with arbitrary small error, or vice versa. Every layered Hopfield neural network has a fuzzy logical framework of the q-value weighted bounded operator with arbitrary small error. This means that if the sigmoid function used by Hopfield neurons is a piecewise linear function, such kind leveled fuzzy granular system is structure keeping. Unfortunately, if the sigmoid function is the logistic function, such kind leveled fuzzy granular system is usually not structure keeping. Only in an approximate case(see Sigmoid function and Logic), a layered Hopfield neural network may have a structure keeping leveled fuzzy granular system.

4.2.2 Three Important Theorems about the Possibility of Simulating Fuzzy Granular Computing in a Layered Dynamical Neural Networks

In this chapter, we show that Hopfield neural networks can accord with fuzzy logic perfectly, so above mentioned fuzzy logical granular computing can be realized by Hopfield neural networks. For more, we prove that Hopfield neural networks can simulate almost all neuron models, so **theoretically speaking, granular computing can be viewed as a very good information processing framework for almost all neural models.**

H D I Abarbanel et al (1996) [1] studied the synchronization of 13 neuron models. These models include [6, 9–11, 13, 16, 22, 26, 30, 46, 48, 61] and integrate-and-fire model [7][see Eq. (4.9), the rest 11 neuron models are all the special cases of the generalized model described by the ordinary differential equation (4.11).

$$\ddot{x}_i + \mu(x_{ai}^2 - p^2)\dot{x}_i + g^2 x_{ai} = f(t).$$
$$x_{ai} = x_i + \sum_j \lambda_{ji} x_j \tag{4.7}$$

$$\dot{x}_i = y_i,$$
$$\dot{y}_i + \mu(x_{ai}^2 - p^2)y_i + g^2 x_{ai} = f(t).$$
$$x_{ai} = x_i + \sum_j \lambda_{ji} x_j \tag{4.8}$$

$$\frac{dv}{dt} = -\frac{v}{\tau_0} + x_{ext} + x_{syn}(t) \tag{4.9}$$

Where $0 < v < \Theta$ and $v(t_0^+) = 0 \, \text{if} \, v(t_0^-) = \Theta$. Usually $x_{syn}(t)$ is defined by Eq. (4.10).

$$I_{syn}(t) = g \sum_{spikes} f(t - t_{spike})$$
$$f(t) = A[\exp(-\tfrac{t}{\tau_1}) - \exp(-\tfrac{t}{\tau_2})] \tag{4.10}$$

In fact, if we introduce a new variable $y_i = \dot{x}_i$, the Van-der-Pol generator [13] model can be changed to Eq. (4.8) which is just a special case of Eq. (4.11); for the integrate-and-fire model, if we use logistic function $\frac{1}{1+\exp(-\lambda(x-T))}$ to replace the step function, the integrate-and-fire model can also has the form of the Eq. (4.11). So the Eq. (4.11) can be viewed as a general representation of almost all neuron models, if we can prove the Eq. (4.11) can be simulated by a neural network based on the Hopfield neuron model[see Eq. (4.1)], then almost all neuron models can be simulated in the same way.

$$\begin{cases} \dot{x}_1 = -a_1 x_1 + w_1 f_1(x_1, x_2, ..., x_n) + u_1 \\ \dot{x}_2 = -a_2 x_2 + w_2 f_2(x_1, x_2, ..., x_n) + u_2 \\ \quad \vdots \\ \dot{x}_n = -a_n x_n + w_n f_n(x_1, x_2, ..., x_n) + u_n \end{cases} \tag{4.11}$$

Where every $f_i(x_1, x_2, ..., x_n), 1 \leq i \leq n$, has the continuous partial differential $\frac{\partial f_i}{\partial x_i}$ in the finite hypercubic domain $D = [a_1, b_1] \times [a_2, b_2] \times ... \times [a_n, b_n]$ of its trajectory space $TR = \{(x_1(t), x_2(t), ..., x_n(t)) : 0 \leq t \leq T\}$.

Eq. (3.6) in above mentioned theorem 2 is the fixed point of a Hopfield neural circuit which only has one cell with input I_k. At the fixed point, every neuron works just like a neuron in a perception neural network. Theorem 1 tries to show the condition of Eq. (3.6) to simulate disjunctive normal form(DNF) formula. The fixed point of Eq (3.6) can easily simulate binary logical operators; on the other hand, a layered neural network can be simulated by a q-value weighted fuzzy logical function. If the neural network described by Eq. (4.1) has a layered structure, the fixed point of a neuron at the non-input layer l is

$$U_{l,i} = \sum_k w_{l,i,k} V_{l-1,i}/a_i$$
$$V_{l,i} = S(U_{l,i} - T)$$

(4.12)

It is easy to know that in the case of single neuron Eq. (4.12) can be simplified into Eq. (3.6), so Hopfield neural networks have high ability to simulate fuzzy logical operator, and can be used in GrC. Eq. (4.12) is just a perception neural network, so a perception neural network can be viewed as an abstract of static points or stable states of a real neural network described by Eq. (4.12).

Theorem 3 shows the fact that every continuous function can be simulated by a layered Hopfield neural network just like a multi layered perception neural network with arbitrary small error. So layered neural networks can complete any task of feature abstracting in visual perception, if the task of of feature abstracting can be represented by a continuous function. Theorem 3 is directly from the universal approximation theorem [24, 37]'s proof.

Theorem 3 *If $f(x_1, \ldots, x_m)$ is a continuous mapping from $[0, 1]^m$ to $(0, 1)^p$, for any $\epsilon > 0$, we can build a layered neural network Ψ which is defined by Eq. (4.12) and has at least two layers, then its fixed point can be viewed as a continuous map*

$$F(x_1, \ldots, x_m) = (F_1(x_1, \ldots, x_m), \ldots, F_q(x_1, \ldots, x_m))$$

from $[0, 1]^m$ to $(0, 1)^p$, and $|F(x_1, \ldots, x_m) - f(x_1, \ldots, x_m)| < \varepsilon$, here $x_1, x_2, \ldots, x_m$ are k inputs of the neural network. For more, for an arbitrary layered neural network Ψ defined by Eq. (4.12) which has a fixed point function $F(x_1, \ldots, x_m)$, we can find a q-value fuzzy logical function $F'(x_1, \ldots, x_m) = (F_1'(x_1, \ldots, x_m), m, F_q'(x_1, \ldots, x_m))$ of weighted Bounded operator , such that

$$|F(x_1, \ldots, x_m) - F'(x_1, \ldots, x_m)| < \varepsilon.$$

Theorem 4 tries to prove that all kind recurrent neural networks described by the Eq. (4.11) can be simulated by Hopfield neural networks described by Eq. (4.1). The ordinary differential Eq. (4.11) has a strong ability to describe neural phenomena. The neural network described by Eq. (4.11)can have feedback. For the sake of the existence of feedback of a recurrent neural network, chaos will occur in such a neural network. As we known, the important characteristics of chaotic dynamics, i.e., aperiodic dynamics in deterministic systems are the apparent irregularity of time traces and the divergence of the trajectories over time (starting from two nearby initial conditions). Any small error in the calculation of a chaotic deterministic system will cause unpredictable divergence of the trajectories over time, i.e. such kind neural networks may behave very differently under different precise calculations. So any small difference between two approximations of a trajectory of a chaotic recurrent neural network may create two totally different approximate results of this trajectory. Fortunately, all animals have only limited life and the domain of trajectories of their neural network are also finite, so for most neuron models, the Lipschitz condition is hold in a real neural system, and in this case, the simulation is possible.

Theorem 4 *If $[0,T]$, $+\infty > T > 0$, is an arbitrary finite time interval, the trajectory of Eq. (4.11) is limited in the finite hypercubic domain $\mathbb{D} = [a_1, b_1] \times [a_2, b_2] \times ... \times [a_n, b_n]$, and every $f_i(x_1, x_2, ..., x_n)$, $1 \leq i \leq n$ in Eq. (4.11) is continuous in the finite domain D of its trajectory space, and accords with the Lipschitz condition, i.e.*

$$\|f_i(X_1) - f_i(X_2)\| \leq L \cdot \|X_1 - X_2\|, \ 1 \leq i \leq n$$

where L is the Lipschitz constant and $X_j = (x^j{}_1, x^j{}_2, ..., x^j{}_n) \in \mathbb{D}, j = 1, 2$, then every neural network NC described by Eq. (4.11) can be simulated by a Hopfield neural network described described by Eq. (4.1) in the time interval $[0, T]$ and the finite domain $\mathbb{D}$ with an arbitrary small error $\varepsilon > 0$.

Proof: We can build a Hopfield neural network HC described by Eq. (4.1) which has n Hopfield neurons $(x_1, \cdots, x_n)$, these Hopfield neurons simulate n neurons in Eq. (4.11). As Hopfield neurons use logistic function as their activation function, Eq. (4.11) should be changed to Eq. (4.13).

$$\begin{cases} \dot{x}_1 = -\alpha_1 \cdot x_1 + w_1 f_1(rs(V_{x_1}), rs(V_{x_2}), ..., rs(V_{xn})) + u_1 \\ \quad V_{x_1} = \frac{1}{(1+\exp(-x_1))}; \\ \dot{x}_2 = -\alpha_2 \cdot x_2 + w_2 f_2(rs(V_{x_1}), rs(V_{x_2}), ..., rs(V_{xn})) + u_2 \\ \quad V_{x_2} = \frac{1}{(1+\exp(-x_2))} \\ \quad \vdots \\ \dot{x}_n = -\alpha_n \cdot x_n + w_n f_n(rs(V_{x_1}), rs(V_{x_2}), ..., rs(V_{x_n})) + u_n \\ \quad V_{x_n} = \frac{1}{(1+\exp(-x_n))}; \end{cases} \qquad (4.13)$$

Where $rs(x) = thr - \ln((1 - x)/x)$ is the reverse function of the logistic function $L(x) = \frac{1}{1+\exp(-x+thr)}$;

Not loosing generality, by selecting suitable w_i and u_j, we can suppose every function $f_i(rs(y_1), rs(y_2), \cdots, rs(y_n))$, is a continuous map from $\mathbb{H} = [L(a_1), L(b_1)] \times [L(a_2), L(b_2)] \times ... \times [L(a_n), L(b_n)]$ to $[0, 1]$, $1 \leq i \leq n$, here $rs(y_i) = x_i$. Because $\mathbb{D} = [a_1, b_1] \times [a_2, b_2] \times \cdots \times [a_n, b_n]$ is a finite hypercubic domain, $\mathbb{H}$ must also be a finite hypercubic domain.

For any $\varepsilon > 0$, according to the universal approximation theorem(Simon Haykin]), given any continuous map $f_q(\cdot)$ on the hypercubic $\mathbb{H}$ to $[0, 1]$, there exists a function $F(y_1, \cdots, y_n) = \sum_{i=1}^{m} \alpha_i^q \varphi(\sum_{j=1}^{n} w_{ij}^q y_j + \beta_i^q)$, such that $F(y_1, \cdots, y_n)$ is an approximate realization of the map $f_q(\cdot)$ with an arbitrary precision ε_1, i.e. $|F_q(y_1, \cdots, y_n) - f_q(rs(y_1), rs(y_2), \cdots, rs(y_n))| < \varepsilon_1$, for all vectors $(y_1, , y_n)$ that lie in the input space.

In an above $F(y_1, \cdots, y_n)$, m is an integer and α_i^q, β_i^q and w_{ij}^q are real constants, $i = \cdots, m$ and $j = 1, \cdots, n$, $0 < \varepsilon_1 << \varepsilon$, $\varphi(\cdot)$ in $F(y_1, \cdots, y_n)$ is a nonconstant, bounded and monotone continuous function, for Hopfield neuron, $\varphi(\cdot)$ is the logistic function.

In this way, $F_q(y_1, \cdots, y_n)$ can be computed by a neural network with m Hopfield neurons. We denote the Hopfield neural network which computes $f_k(rs(y_1), rs(y_2), ..., rs(y_n))$ as Ω_k (see Fig. 4.2). Every neuron φ in Ω_k takes the outputs of n neurons $(x_1, \cdots, x_n)$ as its input. The outputs of all neurons in Ω_k are summed up as $w_k \cdot F_k(y_1, \cdots, y_n) = \sum_{i=1}^{m^K} w_k \cdot a_i^k \varphi(\sum_{j=1}^{n} w_{ij}^k y_j + b_i^k)$ (see Fig. 4.2) and feed back to the input of the neuron x_k. If $a_i, i = 1, \cdots, n$ are time coefficients in Eq. (4.13), by choosing enough large b_i as the time coefficient of Ω_k, i.e.,

Page 33

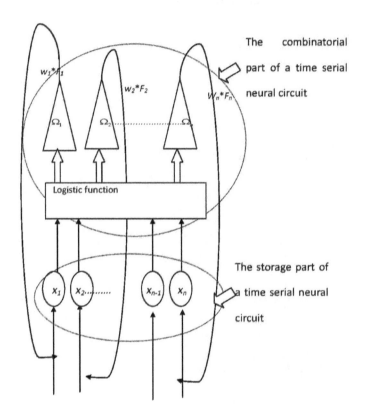

Figure 4.2: Every neural circuit described by Eq. (4.11) is a time serial neural circuit and can be simulated by a Hopfield neural circuit with arbitrary small error. Here each Ω_i is a layered neural circuit which considers $f_i(x_1, x_2, ..x_n)$ as its output at its fixed point.

$b_i >> \max_{1 \le i \le n} (a_i)$, the feedback will be fast enough.

Because $\mathbb{D}$ is closed and every $f_i(x_1, x_2, ..., x_n), 1 \le i \le n$, is a continuous and bounded function in the domain $\mathbb{D}$, and accords with the Lipschitz condition every $f_i(x_1, x_2, ..., x_n), 1 \le i \le n$, according to the Cauchy-Lipschitz Theorem, for a definite initial condition $X(0) = (x_1(0), x_2(0), ..., x_n(0))$, the neural network NC described by Eq. (4.13) has one and only one continuous trajectory $X_{NC}(t) = (x_1^{NC}(t), x_2^{NC}(t), ..., x_n^{NC}(t)) = F_{NC}(t)$, here $F_{NC} : R \to R^n$.

Similarly, when starts at same initial condition $X(0)$, the neural network HC simulating the Eq. (4.13) also has one and only one continuous trajectory

$$X_{HC}(t) = (x_1^{HC}(t), x_2^{HC}(t), ..., x_n^{HC}(t)) = F_{HC}(t),$$

here $F_{HC} : R \to R^n$.

Based on above analysis, the difference $F_{NC}(t) - F_{HC}(t)$ can be described by Eq. (4.14).

$$F_{NC}(t_1) - F_{HC}(t_1) =$$
$$\int_0^{t_1} \left(\dot{x}_1^{NC}(t) - \dot{x}_1^{HC}(t), \dot{x}_2^{NC}(t) - \dot{x}_2^{HC}(t), ..., \dot{x}_n^{NC}(t) - \dot{x}_n^{HC}(t) \right) dt \qquad (4.14)$$
$$= \int_0^{t_1} \left(\eta_1(x_1(t), x_2(t), ..., x_n(t)), \eta_2(x_1(t), x_2(t), ..., x_n(t)), ..., \eta_n(x_1(t), x_2(t), ..., x_n(t)) \right) dt$$

Where

$$|\eta_i(x_1(t), x_2(t), ..., x_n(t))|$$
$$= |F_i(L(x_1(t)), ..., L(x_n(t))) - f_i(x_1(t), ..., x_n(t))| < \varepsilon_1, \quad i = 1, ..., n.$$

So the difference of the trajectories between NC and HC described by Eq. (4.13) can be smaller than ε, if we select an enough small $\varepsilon_1, 0 < \varepsilon_1 << \varepsilon$. In fact, we can prove that

$$err_G \le nT \cdot \varepsilon_1,$$

here

$$err_G = \int_0^T ||F_{NC}(t) - F_{HC}(t)|| dt$$
$$= \int_0^T \sum_{i=1}^n |x_i^{NC}(t) - x_i^{HC}(t)| dt \qquad (4.15)$$

In this way we can use a Hopfield neural network which has a standard structure to simulate an arbitrary neural network defined by Eq. (4.11). □

The condition that every $f_i(x_1, x_2, ..., x_n), 1 \le i \le n$ in Eq. (4.11) is continuous in the finite domain $\mathbb{D}$ can be relax to a piecewise continuous function, the deduction 1 tells this fact.

Deduction 1 Define $X = (x_1, x_2, ..., x_n)$, and $\mathbb{D}$ as the finite hypercubic domain of the trajectory of Eq. (4.11). Suppose in Eq. (4.11), every $f_i(X) = g_i(\phi_i(X))$, here every $g_i(x) : R \to R$ is a piecewise continuous function, and every $\phi_i(X) : R^n \to R, 1 \le i \le n$ is continuous in the finite domain $\mathbb{D}$, then in an arbitrary finite time interval T_{finite}, the neuron model described by Eq. (4.11) can be simulated by a Hopfield neural network with arbitrary precision.

Proof. For every $\phi_i(X)$ is continuous and every $g_i(x)$ is a piecewise continuous function, we can define N_i

intervals : $T_{l,r}^i : |x - x_l^i| < r$, $l = 1, 2, N_i$, here $P_{S_i} = (x_1^i, x_2^i, ..., x_{N_i}^i)$ is a finite set of points, which accords with $x_p^i > x_q^i, p > q$, for any enough small $0 < r$.

It is easy to know the following conditions are permitted for every $g_i(\phi_i(X))$:

(1) Every$\phi_i(X), 1 \leq i \leq n$ is continuous in the finite domain $\mathbb{D}$ of its trajectory space, and accords with the Lipschitz condition, i.e.

$$\|\phi_i(X_1) - \phi_i(X_2)\| \leq L \cdot \|X_1 - X_2\|, \ 1 \leq i \leq n$$

where L is the Lipschitz constant and $X_j = (x^j{}_1, x^j{}_2, ..., x^j{}_n) \in \mathbb{D}$, $j = 1, 2$, (2) If T is the interval T : $(\min\limits_{X \in \mathbb{D}} (\phi_i(X)), \max\limits_{X \in \mathbb{D}} (\phi_i(X)))$, every $g_i(x), 1 \leq i \leq n$ is bounded in T, for more, every$g_i(x), 1 \leq i \leq n$ is continuous and accords with the Lipschitz condition in every interval of the domain $T - \bigcup\limits_{1 \leq l \leq N_i} T_{l,r}^i$.

Suppose $S_r = \{r_i : r_i > 0\}$ is a set of positive reals, and $\lim\limits_{i \to \infty} r_i \to 0$.

For every $g_i(x), 1 \leq i \leq n$ in Eq. (4.11), define a function series

$$S_{g_i} = \{g_i{}^k(x) : k = 1, 2, ...\},$$

where the definition of $g_i{}^k(x)$ is as bellow:

$$g_i{}^k(x) = \begin{cases} g_i(x), \ x \in T - \bigcup\limits_{1 \leq l \leq N_i} T_{l,r_k}^i \\ g_{l,r_k}^i(x), \ x \in T_{l,r_k}^i, 1 \leq l \leq N_i \end{cases}$$

here $g_{l,r_k}^i(x)$ is defined as:

$$g_{l,r_k}^i(x) = \begin{cases} g_i(x_l^i + r_k), \ x \geq x_l^i + r_k \\ g_i(x_l^i - r_k) + \frac{x - x_l^i + r_k}{2 \cdot r_k} \cdot \left(g_i(x_l^i + r_k) - g_i(x_l^i - r_k)\right), \ x \in T_{l,r_k}^i \\ g_i(x_l^i - r_k), \ x \leq x_l^i - r_k \end{cases}$$

It is easy to know, $g_i{}^k(x)$ is a continuous function in the domain T. Now we try to prove $g_i{}^k(x)$ accords with the Lipschitz condition . If x_1 and x_2 are two points in the interval T, there are three cases:

1. $x_1, x_2 \in T' = (x_{p-1}^i + r_k, x_p^i - r_k)$.

   For no points in P_{S_i} is located in the interval T', according to the condition of this deduction, there is a Lipschitz constant $L1$, such that

   $$|g_i^k(x_1) - g_i^k(x_2)| \leq L_1 \cdot |x_1 - x_2|, \ 1 \leq i \leq n;$$

2. $x_1, x_2 \in \bar{T}_{l,r_k}^i$, here $\bar{T}_{l,r_k}^i$ is just the closed set of T_{l,r_k}^i, i.e, $\bar{T}_{l,r_k}^i : |x - x_l^i| \leq r_k$. In this case, we have :

   $$|g_i(x_1) - g_i(x_2)| = |g_{l,r_k}^i(x_1) - g_{l,r_k}^i(x_2)|$$
   $$= \left| \frac{x_1 - x_2}{2 \cdot r_k} \cdot \left(g_i(x_l^i + r_k) - g_i(x_l^i - r_k)\right) \right|$$
   $$\leq L_2 \cdot |x_1 - x_2|$$

3. $x_1 < x_2$, and between x_1 and x_2 there are a K-points subset P_{Ss_i} of P_{S_i}, i.e., $P_{Ss_i} = (x^i_{j+1}, x^i_{j+2}, ..., x^i_{j+K}) \subseteq P_{S_i}$.

In this case,

$$|g_i(x_1) - g_i(x_2)| \leq$$

$$\left| g_i(x_1) - g_i(x^i_{j+1}) + \sum_{l=1}^{K} \left(g_i(x^i_{j+l}) - g_i(x^i_{j+l+1}) \right) + g_i(x^i_{j+k}) - g_i(x_2) \right|$$

$$\leq |g_i(x_1) - g_i(x^i_{j+1})| + \sum_{l=1}^{K} \left| \left(g_i(x^i_{j+l}) - g_i(x^i_{j+l+1}) \right) \right| + |g_i(x^i_{j+k}) - g_i(x_2)|$$

$$\leq L_1|x_1 - x^i_{j+1}| + L_2 \sum_{l=1}^{K} \left| x^i_{j+l} - x^i_{j+l+1} \right| + L_1|x^i_{j+k} - x_2|$$

$$\leq L \cdot |x_1 - x_2|$$

Where $L = \max(L_1, L_2)$.

Based on above facts, $g_i{}^k(x)$ accords with the Lipschitz condition. Now define $f_i^k(X) = g_i^k(\phi_i(X))$, for all $k = 1, 2 \cdots$, substituting $f_i(X)$ by $f_i^k(X)$ in Eq. (4.11) we have

$$\begin{cases} \dot{x}_1 = -a_1 x_1 + w_1 f_1^k(x_1, x_2, ..., x_n) + u_1 \\ \dot{x}_2 = -a_2 x_2 + w_2 f_2^k(x_1, x_2, ..., x_n) + u_2 \\ \quad \vdots \\ \dot{x}_n = -a_n x_n + w_n f_n^k(x_1, x_2, ..., x_n) + u_n \end{cases} \tag{4.16}$$

Define the neural network described by Eq. (4.16) as NC_k. Based on the theorem 4, the neural network described byEq. (4.16) can be simulated by a Hopfield neural network HC_k with arbitrary small error. For a definite initial condition

$$X(0) = (x_1(0), x_2(0), ..., x_n(0)),$$

according to the Cauchy-Lipschitz Theorem, every neural network NC_k has one and only one continuous trajectory

$$X_{NC_k}(t) = (x_1^{NC_k}(t), x_2^{NC_k}(t), ..., x_n^{NC_k}(t)) = F_{NC_k}(t)$$

and every neural network HC_k has also one and only one continuous trajectory

$$X_{HC_k}(t) = (x_1^{HC_k}(t), x_2^{HC_k}(t), ..., x_n^{HC_k}(t)) = F_{HC_k}(t).$$

At other hand, if for the same initial condition

$$X(0) = (x_1(0), x_2(0), ..., x_n(0)),$$

the neural network NC described by Eq. (4.11) has a trajectory

$$X_{NC}(t) = (x_1^{NC}(t), x_2^{NC}(t), ..., x_n^{NC}(t)) = F_{NC}(t),$$

here $F_{NC}: R \rightarrow R^n$.

The difference $F_{NC}(t) - F_{NC_k}(t)$ can be described by following equation:

$$F_{NC}(t_1) - F_{NC_k}(t_1) =$$

$$\int_0^{t_1} \left(\dot{x}_1^{NC}(t) - \dot{x}_1^{NC_k}(t), \dot{x}_2^{NC}(t) - \dot{x}_2^{NC_k}(t), ..., \dot{x}_n^{NC}(t) - \dot{x}_n^{NC_k}(t) \right) dt$$

$$= \int_0^{t_1} \left(\eta_1(x_1(t), x_2(t), ..., x_n(t)), \eta_2(x_1(t), x_2(t), ..., x_n(t)), ..., \eta_n(x_1(t), x_2(t), ..., x_n(t)) \right) dt$$

Where

$$\eta_i(x_1(t), x_2(t), ..., x_n(t)) = f_i(X(t)) - f_i^k(X(t)) = 0,$$

when

$$\phi_i(x_1^{NC}(t), x_2^{NC}(t), ..., x_n^{NC}(t)), \phi_i(x_1^{NC_k}(t), x_2^{NC_k}(t), ..., x_n^{NC_k}(t)) \in T - \bigcup_{1 \leq l \leq N_i} T_{l,r_k}^i;$$

and otherwise, $|\eta_i(x_1(t), x_2(t), ..., x_n(t))| < M$ for $f_i(X)$ and $f_i^k(X)$ are bounded for all $i = 1, ..., n$.

So

$$|F_{NC}(t_1) - F_{NC_k}(t_1)|$$

$$\leq M \cdot \int_{t \notin \phi_i(x_1^{NC}(t), x_2^{NC}(t),...,x_n^{NC}(t)), \phi_i(x_1^{NC_k}(t), x_2^{NC_k}(t),...,x_n^{NC_k}(t)) \in T - \bigcup_{1 \leq l \leq N_i} T_{l,r_k}^i} \sqrt{n} \cdot dt$$

When $\lim_{k \to \infty} r_k \to 0$, $T - \bigcup_{1 \leq l \leq N_i} T_{l,r_k}^i \Rightarrow T$, the length of trajectory of $F_{NC}(t)$(or $F_{NC_k}(t)$) in the region $\phi_i(x_1^{NC}(t), x_2^{NC}(t), \cdots, x_n^{NC}(t)) \in T_{l,r_k}^i$, $i = 1, 2, \cdots, n, l = 1, 2, \cdots, N_i$, also trends to zero, the reason for this is that the length of trajectory of $F_{NC}(t)$ (or $F_{NC_k}(t)$) is limited for the time interval T_{finite} is finite. So $|F_{NC}(t_1) - F_{NC_k}(t_1)|$ can be smaller than any $\varepsilon > 0$. Base on above two facts, a neural network NC defined by Eq. (4.11) can be simulated by Hopfield neural network HC_k with arbitrary small error, when r_k is small enough or k is large enough.□

According to the deduction 1, we can prove many neural models can be simulated by Hopfield neural model, e.g. the dynamics of the generalized brain-state-in-a-box (GBSB neural model) [21] is described by the following state equation:

$$X(k+1) = G(X(k) + \alpha \cdot (W \cdot X(k) + B)))$$

where $X(k) \in R^n$ is the state vector at time k, α is step size, W is the weight matrix, b is a bias vector, and $G(X) = (g_1(X), \cdots, g_n(X)) : R^n \rightarrow R^n$ is a linear saturating function whose ith component is a function defined as follows:

$$g_i(X = \{x_1, x_2, ..., x_i, ..., x_n\}) = \begin{cases} 1, & \text{if } x_i > 1 \\ x_i, & \text{if } 1 \geq x_i \geq -1 \\ -1, & \text{if } x_i < -1 \end{cases}$$

Changing above discrete dynamics of the $GBSB$ model to the continuous model, we have :

$$X(t + dt) - X(t) = (G(x(t) + \alpha \cdot (W \cdot X(t) + B))) - X(t)) \cdot dt,$$

i.e.

$$\begin{cases} \dot{x}_1 = -x_1 + f_1(x_1, x_2, ..., x_n) \\ \dot{x}_2 = -x_2 + f_2(x_1, x_2, ..., x_n) \\ \qquad\qquad \vdots \\ \dot{x}_n = -x_n + f_n(x_1, x_2, ..., x_n) \end{cases}$$

Where every $f_i(x_1, x_2, \cdots, x_n) = g(x(k) + \alpha \cdot (W \cdot x(k) + b)))$ is continuous and bounded in its traject space and accords with the Lipschitz condition, so the $GBSB$ model can be simulated by a Hopfield neural network according to the above deduction.

Deduction 2: For a neuron model N, if the fixed point of its neuron can be viewed as a nonconstant, bounded and monotone continuous function of input, i.e. the output y of a neuron can be described by $y = f_{fix}(I)$ at its fixed point and $f_{fix}()$ is a nonconstant, bounded and monotone continuous function of I, then every neural network NC described by Eq. (4.11) can be simulated by a neural network of this neuron model N in an arbitrary finite time interval $[0, T]$ with an arbitrary small error $\varepsilon > 0$.

Proof. We can prove this deduction by simply replacing the logistic function by $f_{fix}()$ in the proof of above Theorem 2.$\square$

If we set the coefficients in RH model [see Eq. (4.17)] as $a = -1$, $b = c = d = r = s = 0$, The RH function will degenerate to the equation

$$\dot{x} = e^{-t} - x^3 + I_{stim},$$

when time t trends to infinite, x has a fixed point $x = \sqrt[3]{I_{stim}}$ which is a nonconstant, bounded and monotone continuous function of input, so in this degenerated case, RH neural network can simulate all neural networks NC described by Eq. (4.11). Simulating the Rose-Hindmarsh (RH) model neuron by a Hopfield neural network. RH model consists of a system of three coupled nonlinear first-order differential equations which can be used to describe the bursting behavior of certain neurons(Hindmash J L. and Rose R M. [9]). The Eq. (4.17) is the differential equation of RH model .

$$\begin{aligned} \dot{x} &= y + ax^3 - bx^2 - z + I_{stim} \\ \dot{y} &= c - dx^2 - y \\ \dot{z} &= r\left[s\left(x - x_0\right) - z\right] \end{aligned} \qquad (4.17)$$

where x stands for the membrane potential, y is the fast recovery currents, z describes slow adaptive currents, and I_{stim} means the afferent input current, a, b, c, d, r, s, x_0 are constants. In Eq. (4.17), the membrane potential x may go to infinite under some parameters, but for a real biochemical system, a RH neuron can never have an infinite trajectory. So Eq. (4.17) can be simulated by a Hopfield neural network according to the Theorem 2 under the finite trajectory condition.

In this book, the parameter $a = 1, b = 3, c = 1, d = 5, s = 4, r = 0.015$, and $x_0 = -1.6$. For the Rose-Hindmarsh neuron, the time scale is defined as 5 units of Eq. (4.17) equaling 1 ms. In order to simulate RH model, we change

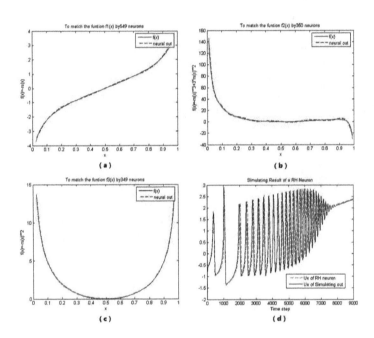

Figure 4.3: The key to simulate a RH neuron by a Hopfield neural network lies in the perfect simulation of the three function $f_1(x)$, $f_2(x)$ and $f_3(x)$. The simulation results are showed in (a),(b) and (c) respectively. (d) is the simulation result of a RH neuron. The dash line is the electromotive force u_x of the RH neuron and the solid line is the corresponding u_x of simulating.

Eq. (4.17) to Eq. (4.18)

$$\dot{u}_x = -u_x + (a \cdot rs(v_x)^3 - b \cdot rs(v_x)^2 - rs(v_z) + rs(v_y) + rs(v_x)) + I_{stim}$$
$$v_x = \frac{1}{(1+exp(-u_x))};$$
$$\dot{u}_y = -u_y + c - d \cdot rs(v_x)^2$$
$$v_y = \frac{1}{(1+exp(-u_y))};$$
$$\dot{u}_z = -r \cdot u_z + r\left[s\left(rs(v_x) - x_0\right)\right]$$
$$v_z = \frac{1}{(1+exp(-u_z))};$$

(4.18)

Where $rs(x) = -\ln((1-x)/x)$ is the reverse function of the logistic function.

According to the Theorem 4, it is easy to see that the key to simulate Eq. (4.18) by Hopfield model neurons is to simulate the three functions $f_1(x) = rs(x)$, $f_2(x) = a \cdot rs(x)^3 - b \cdot rs(x)^2$ and $f_3(x) = rs(x)^2$. The $f_1(x)$, $f_2(x)$ and $f_3(x)$ are simulated by Ω_1 with 549 neurons, Ω_2 with 350 neurons and Ω_3 with 349 neurons respectively. The simulating result shows that a 1251 neurons Hopfield neural network can simulate a RH neuron perfectly (see Fig. 4.3.). The coefficients are learned by a new Back propagation approach. In order to enhance the efficiency of Back Propagation learning, we propose a novel approach denoted as Back propagation vector machine (LPSVM) which combine BP approach with Support vector machine. Support vector machines (Vapnik, Esther Levin ,Yann Le Cun, 1994) [58] learn classifiers which maximize the margin of the classification: An input $Z_k \in R^d$ is classified by $sign(\alpha \cdot Z_k)$, and α is calculated such that for all training examples Z_k the dot product $|\alpha \cdot Z_k|$ is large. As the learning approach is not the main point of this book, we only simply introduce our approach. In the Theorem 4, every Hopfield neural network Ω_k which computes $f_k(rs(y_1), rs(y_2), ..., rs(y_n))$ has two layers weights, in our algorithm, the output layers weights is computed by psvm(Fung G. Mangasarian O [5]) approach and the input layers weight is computed by ordinary Bp approach. Neural networks described by Eq. (4.11) can include almost all neural models found nowadays. We uses 1251 neurons Hopfield neural network to simulate a Rose-Hindmarsh (RH) neuron. Rose-Hindmarsh (RH) neuron is much more complicate than Hopfield neurons. To simulate a complicate neuron by simple neurons is not a difficult task, but the reverse task is almost impossible to complete, i.e., it is almost impossible to simulate a Hopfield neuron by a set of RH neurons.

Chapter 5

Designing of Dynamic Neural System

In above chapter, we have discussed the problem of designing the steady state of a layered neural network as a granular computing. Traditional views of visual processing suggest that early visual neurons in areas V1 and V2 are static spatiotemporal filters that extract local features from a visual scene. The extracted information is then channeled through a feedforward chain of modules in successively higher visual areas for further analysis. Recent electrophysiological recordings from early visual neurons in awake behaving monkeys reveal that there are many levels of complexity in the information processing of the early visual cortex, as seen in the long-latency responses of its neurons. so in the neural science, the design of nonlinear dynamic neural circuits to model bioneural experimental results is also an important and intricate task. In this chapter, we simply discuss the problem of how designing a dynamic neural system. There are two approaches for designing a dynamic neural network. The first way tries to combine several layered neural networks, which complete several tasks of granular computing at their static states. The second way tries to use the approaches used in designing of digital computers.

5.1   Dynamical Neural Granular Computing Assemply

Visual cognition under selective attention is a hot topic in image understanding. Large-scale hierarchical systems for object detection using bottom-up (signal-driven) processing results with top-down (model or task-driven) attentional modulation are designed for this purpose. Granular systems can be used to develop such kind large-scale hierarchical systems. The bottom-up data flow proceeds from a preprocessing level to the hypothesis level where object hypotheses created by exhaustive object detection algorithms are represented in a roughly retinotopic way.

Just as Gepperth A R T et.al.(2011) [19] pointed out that a competitive selection mechanism is used to determine the most confident hypotheses, which are used on the system level to train multimodal models that link object identity to invariant hypothesis properties. The top-down data flow originates at the system level, where the trained multimodal models are used to obtain space- and feature-based attentional modulation signals, providing biases for the competitive selection process at the hypothesis level. This results in object-specific hypothesis facilitation/suppression in certain image regions which we show to be applicable to different object detection mechanisms.

We firstly training several layered neural networks for the detection of certain objects, e.g. cars, then a com-

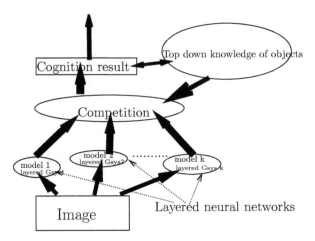

Figure 5.1: When one of Statical Gsyses finds an object in a granule accords with it, it transmits exciting signals to other static Gsyses of the same kind, and inhibiting signals to inhomogeneou static Gsyses.

petition neural network, which is guided by top down knowledge of objects, is built for competitive selection mechanism, which is used to determine the most confident hypotheses for objects cognition. There is a feed back from competition result and object knowledge base (Fig. 5.1).

The competition network cooperates with the object knowledge base that the recurrent feedforward/feedback loops in the cortex serve to integrate top-down contextual priors and bottom-up observations so as to implement concurrent probabilistic inference along the visual hierarchy. For example, in order to recognize a face in an image, if a layered $Gsys_i$, which is in charge of recognizing an eye, wins the competition and has a higher competition output than other layered $Gsys$es, then the object knowledge base will activate a rule to recognize a face , this rule will send a series exciting messages to all friendly layered $Gsys$es about mouth,nose,ear, etc. for the purpose of recognizing a face. Exciting messages can be sent to enhance the time coefficients a_i in Eq. (4.1) of a layered $Gsys$ to accelerate convergence of the corresponding layered neural network .

The benefits of such kind approaches are proved by Gepperth A R T et.al in the task for detecting of cars in a variety of challenging traffic videos. Gepperth A R T et.al [19] have evaluated their approach on a publicly available data set containing approximately 3,500 annotated video images from more than 1h of driving, they have shown strong increases in performance and generalization when compared to object detection in isolation. Furthermore, they compared their results to a late hypothesis rejection approach, showing that early coupling of top-down and bottom-up information is a favorable approach especially when processing resources are constrained.

The technique used in designing time series's digit circuits can be used in the designing of a neural network with feedback. The following section discusses this technique.

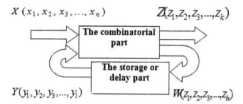

$X(x_1, x_2, x_3, \ldots, x_n)$ $Z(z_1, z_2, z_3, \ldots, z_k)$

The combinatorial part

The storage or delay part

$Y(y_1, y_2, y_3, \ldots, y_i)$ $W(z_1, z_2, z_3, \ldots, z_h)$

Figure 5.2: A time serial electronic digit circuit has a structure with two parts combinatorial part and storage part

5.2 Designing Dynamical Neural network as a Digit Circuit

Under the help of fuzzy logic, we can design neural models similar to design binary digit circuits. Binary digit circuits' design is started from basic functional blocks which can be found in every handbook of digital circuits. The similar approach can be used by the design of a neural circuit. Electronic digit circuits can be classified as combinatorial circuits and time serial circuits. Neural circuits can also be classified into similar two kind neural circuits-combinatorial neural circuits and time serial neural circuits.

Combinatorial neural circuits: A circuit is defined as combinatorial neural circuit if its output at time t is determined by the inputs at time t.

Time serial neural circuits: A circuit is defined as a time serial neural circuit if its output at time t and the next state $S(t+1)$ are determined not only by the inputs at time t, but also by the neural circuits state at time t, $S(t)$, and before time t. It is easy to show that combinatorial neural circuits have layered structure and time serial circuits have recurrent structure. A time serial electronic digit circuit has a structure with two parts combinatorial part and storage part, we also restrict the structure of a time serial neural circuit in a similar structure showed in Fig 5.2. We have proved in the theorem 4 that all kind neural circuits which have recurrent structure can be simulated by a time serial neural circuit described by a Hopfield neural network described described by Eq. (4.1) with arbitrary small error. In Fig 5.2, the function of a complicate time serial neural circuit can be described by input X, output Z and inner output Z and inner input W. The relations of them are $Z(t_n) = F[X(tn), Y(tn)]$ (the output of the whole circuit), $W(t_n) = G[X(tn), Y(tn)]$ (the storage inspiring function), and $Y(t_{n+1}) = H[X(tn), W(tn)]$ (the storage state function).

The most elementary combinatorial neural circuits are: 1. $\wedge$ and gate, 2. $\vee$ or gate, 3. $\rightarrow$ not gate, 4. delay gate. For delay gate $\square$, output (Fig. 5.3).

According to the theorem 2, a Hopfield neuron can simulate above 4 elementary gates. Suppose the output at the fixed point is $v_i(\cdot)$, $v_i(\cdot)$ is defined as high if $v_i(\cdot) \geq t_i$ and defined as low if $v_i(\cdot) < t_i$. For two inputs x_1, x_2, a similar definition is also proposed.

The fuzzy logical framework of above elementary combinatorial neural circuits has following characters:

And gate Set $\alpha = 1$. If $w_{ik} > \varepsilon > 0$, we select suitable t_i and ε such that $v_i(\cdot)$ is high, iff x_1 and x_2 are both high;

Or gate Set $\alpha = 1$. If $w_{ik} > \varepsilon > 0$ we select suitable t_i and ε such that $v_i(\cdot)$ is high, iff one of x_1 and x_2 is high.

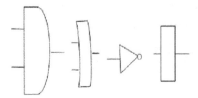

Figure 5.3: The four elementary combinatorial neural circuits are: 1. $\bigwedge$ and gate, 2. $\bigvee$or gate, 3. $\rightharpoondown$ not gate, 4. $\square$ delay gate.

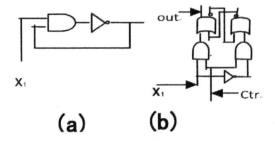

Figure 5.4: (a) oscillator; (b)register

Not gate$w_{i1} < \varepsilon < 0$and $w_{i2} = 1$the input of x_2 is 1. We select suitable t_i and ε such that $v_i(\cdot)$ is high, iff x_1 is low ,and $v_i(\cdot)$ is high is low, iff x_1 is high;

Delay gate: Set $T_i = 0$, $w_{i1} = 0$ and $w_{i2} = 1$. α_i controls the delay from input I_2 to output. Register and oscillator are two elementary circuits for time serial neural circuits. Fig. 5.4(a) is the famous Wilson-Cowan Oscillator (Wilson M A, Cowan J D, 1972) [60], this simplest oscillator is created by one excitatory cell and one initiatory cell. When the input potential increases to a certain level, the output begins to fire pulses. Oscillation is a fundamental function of a neural system. The synchronized oscillations shown in [38] are just completed by a column structure of neural system. In the binary case, a register can dynamically store at least one bit of information, in the fuzzy logical case, a register should be able to store the input $x(t)$, when the control pulse c comes. So there are two kind ways to store information in a neural circuit: (1) to store information in weights by some kind learning approaches, (3) to store information in registers. The simplest fuzzy register is shown in Fig. 5.4(b).

Chapter 6

Granular System for Visual Task

The columnar organization of our brain's primary visual cortex strongly supports the granular system defined aforementioned. Many functions of the primary visual cortex are still unknown, but the columnar organization is well understood. The lateral geniculate nucleus (LGN) transfers information from eyes to brain stem and primary visual cortex (V1) [47] . Columnar organization of V1 plays an important role in the processing of visual information.

Local similarity of information processing gives rise to Columnar organization has a granular structure. V1 is composed of a grid of $(1 \times 1mm^2)$ neural area of hypercolumns(hc) in our brain's primary visual cortex. Every hypercolumn contains a set of minicolumns(mc), which have same focus. Each hypercolumn analyzes information from one small region(described by a distance function) of the retina. Adjacent hypercolumns analyze information from adjacent areas of the retina, so the structure of a columnar organization can be described by a set of fuzzy logical formulas similar to a granular system. Hypercolumns(or supercolumns), minicolumns(mc) can be viewed as granules. Similar to the primary visual cortex, in our granular system, there are two kind granules:hyper-granule and mini-granules in some levels of our granular system. A hyper-granule contain a bundle of mini-granules.

Definition 13 *[Perception Granular system of Columnar Organization(COGsys)] A perception columnar organization is a special perception granular system, in which, there is at least one hyper-granule $G(coeG^{n+1})$ such that all mini-granules included in it have same convex region, but different adjoint functions.*

In this chaper, in order to simulating visual cortex, a granular system of columnar organization(COGsys) is designed for the image-matting task. In our Hybrid designing approach(LPSVM), we firstly design Leveled Granular Systems with the help of fuzzy logic, and then we use PSVM to accomplish the learning for some concrete visual tasks.

6.1 The Leveled Granular Computing for Perception Purpose

In this section we discuss the problem of information sampling and granular processing for perception cognition, and we consider image matting as an example.

Our universe is a complex, chaotic dynamical system. As we know information displays in a fractal way in a complex, chaotic dynamical system, i.e. when we zoom in, infinite small detailed structure of nature will be continuously explored before us, when we zoom out, infinite large structure of nature will be continuously displayed before us. The information of nature is continuous and incomputable under the meaning of the classical Turing machine. From the engineer point of view or from computable point of view, the information from nature should be sampled approximately, and only countable or finite sensors can be settled in our environment by us. The sensors distributed in our environment should be distributed in a grid way.

The size of a sensors' grid can be determined according to the famous Shannon-Whittaker theorem about information sampling. Shannon-Whittaker theorem says that if $\hat{f}$ is the Fourier transformation of a signal f and $\hat{f}$ has a support set $[-\pi/T, \pi/T]$, then f can be recovered by the sampling sequence $f(nT)\delta(t-nT), n = 0, 1, 2, 3, ...,$ here δ (x)is an impulse response function (IRF). The restriction that $\hat{f}$ has a support set $[-\pi/T, \pi/T]$ makes $f(x)$ changes smoothly and can be reconstruct by $f(x) = \sum_{i=-\infty}^{+\infty} f(nT)h_\tau(t-nT)$, here $h_\tau(t) = \sin(nt/T)/\pi t/T$. The sampled examples can be represented as matrix, e.g. an image is a two dimensional matrix.

Generally speaking, there are three stages from perception to recognition:

1. Big data information sampling;

2. bridging the gap between detected physical information and semantic information;

3. cognition navigation based on purpose or intent.

The technique of graph-preserving criterion can be used to bridging the gap between detected physical information and semantic information. Generally speaking, the information similarity, proximity and functionality can be described by the graph embedding model. Just as Shuicheng Yan et. Al.(2007) [55] pointed out a large family of algorithms-supervised or unsupervised; stemming from statistics or geometry theory can be unified in a general formulation known as graph embedding. Graph embedding tries to define an intrinsic graph to be the graph **G** itself and a penalty graph $\mathbf{G}_p = \{\mathbb{X}, \mathbb{W}^p\}$ as a graph whose vertices X are just samples and the same as those of **G**, but whose edge weight matrix $\mathbb{W}^p$ corresponds to the similarity characteristics that are to be suppressed. In this paper, we extend the the graph-preserving criterion in [55] as follows:

$$F_O(X_i, \mathbb{W})^T \cdot \mathbb{L} \cdot F_O(X_i, \mathbb{W}) + \min_{\mathbb{W}} \| C_i - F_O(X_i, \mathbb{W}) \|^2 + \lambda \| \mathbb{W} \|$$

(6.1)

here $\mathbb{L}$ is the matrix of the penalty graph, C_i can be viewed as a label or a goal, and $\mathbb{W}$ is a parameter vectors' set. $F_O(X, \mathbb{W})$ is an adjoint function of a granular system.

Generally speaking, there may be many stages of intermediate processing from the input X to $F_O(X, \mathbb{W})$,i.e.

$$F_O(X, \mathbb{W}) = F(F_1(F_2....F_k(X, W_K)), W_2), W_1),$$

where $F_l(X_i, W_l), l = 1, \cdots, K$, is an intermediate adjoint feature vector.

In this chapter, we consider image understanding as an example to show that above mentioned cognition procession can be completed in a framework of granular deep learning. An image is just a 2-dimensional matrix which is sampled from environment. The granular system upon an image is a multi scale information processing system of image understanding.

What is the image understanding? Of course, the image understanding means to find the meaning or content for images. If every color r,g, or b has 256 grades , the number N of color images with size $n \times m$ is tremendous, such that $N = (24 \times m \times n)^{256}$. At other hand, the meaning of an image can be represented by a very small set of labels. The processing of image understanding is just the task of summarizing the tremendous information of images into a small set of labels. Now the problem is that how can we complete the task of feature abstraction done by $F_O(X_i, \mathbf{W})$ in Eq. (6.1)?

In fact, the so called feature abstraction is just a task to eliminate high-order correlation and maintain enough resolution for cognition. The approach of fenestration is a very effective approach. In a multi scale fenestration approach, information abstracting or compressing can be viewed as a processing of extracting useful features by a granular deep learning in a granular system. A frequent used approach of feature extracting for image understanding can be described as two kind steps:

1. Computing the model fitting rate(MFR) of image blocks(small descendant granules) restricted in a small window(a father granule) with a set of pattern models M_s;

2. Computing the probability or frequency(MF)of occurrence of every pattern model M_s in a large image block(forefather granules).

Theoretically speaking, above two kind steps can be reused in a granular system. Above approach has a universal meaning, many approaches can be included in this framework. For example, in signal processing, a finite impulse response (FIR) filter can be completed in this framework. A finite impulse response (FIR) filter is a filter whose impulse response (or response to any finite length input) is of finite duration, because it settles to zero in finite time. This is in contrast to infinite impulse response (IIR) filters, which may have internal feedback and may continue to respond indefinitely (usually decaying).

Now we try to give out a formal description of above two steps. As the level of a GDL is upside down with the level of its $Gsys$, in this section for the sake of simplicity, we consider the level of GDL as a tag of feature vectors or variables, i.e. if there are totally m_{GDL} levels in a $Gsys$, a level $(m_{GDL} - 1) - k = m_{GDL} - (k+1)$ granule has a level k feature vector V^k. For the sake of simplicity, $G(coeG^{m_{GDL}-(k+1)})$ is simplified as $G(coe^k)$, here k is the granular deep learning level. In the following pages, if not obviously pointed out, the word "level" means granular deep learning level.

A set of feature vectors is usually a set of vectors sampled from environment $\mathbb{R}^n$, the information contains in every feature vector can be divided into two parts: the sampling information and the location information, i.e. we can denote a set of feature vectors as

$$I_S = \{V_i^0\} = \{(V_{L,i}^0, V_{I,i}^0)\} = \{(x_{i,1}^0, ..., x_{i,n}^0, v_{i,1}^0, v_{i,1}^0, ..., v_{i,k_0}^0)\},$$

here V_i^0 with a tag 0 means " an adjoint feature vector for a level 0 GDL",
$V_{I,i}^0 = (v_1^0, v_2^0, ..., v_{k_0}^0)$ is the information sensed by a camera, and $V_L^0 = (x_{i,1}^0, ..., x_{i,n}^0)$ is location of a pixel $V_{I,i}^0$ in the space $\mathbb{R}^n$.
For example, an image I can be viewed as a set of pixels $I = \{P_i\} = \{(P_{L,i}^0, P_{I,i}^0)\} = \{(x_{i,1}^0, x_{i,2}^0, r_i, g_i, b_i)\}$, here

$(x_{i,1}^0, x_{i,2}^0)$ is the location of a pixel in the image I, and (r_i, g_i, b_i) is its color values.

According to the definition of $Gsys$ and GDL(see definition 4), for an image I_S, a level $l = (m_{GDL} - 1)$ granule is just I_S itself and a level 0 granule $G(coe^0)$ is just a pixel.

For every granule $G(coe^1)$, $G(coe^1)$ receives information from all $G(coe^0) \in G(coe^1)$, and a new feature vector (*adjoint feature vector*) $V^1 = (V_L^1, V_I^1) = (x_1^1, ..., x_n^1, v_1^1, v_2^1, ..., v_{q_2}^1)$ for $G(coe^1)$ is computed based on all granules $G(coe^0)$ in $G(coe^1)$; generally speaking, every granule $G(coe^{k+1})$ receives information from all $G(coe^k)$ included in it, and a new adjoint feature vector $V^{k+1} = (V_L^{k+1}, V_I^{k+1}) = (x_1^{k+1}, ..., x_n^{k+1}, v_1^{k+1}, v_2^{k+1}, ..., v_{q_{k+1}}^{k+1})$ for $G(coe^{k+1})$ is computed based on all adjoint feature vectors V^k of all granules $G(coe^k)$ included in $G(coe^{k+1})$.

A algorithm with 2 steps of a leveled granular deep learning for the task of adjoint features' computing is proposed here. This algorithm processes three adjoining neighbour layers information of a $Gsys$, and can be repeated along all layers of a $Gsys$.

Algorithm of Adjoint Features' Computing:

In the 1st **step** , the model fitting rate (MFR) of every $k + 1$ level granule $G(coe^{k+1})$, which is a $2^{m_{k+1}}$-dimensional adjoint feature vector $V_{I,G(coe_j^{k+1})}^{k+1}$, can be computed by Eq. (6.2), here we suppose that every granule $G(coe^{k+1})$ has m_{k+1} son granules leveled k (e.g. in the case of an image these son granules can be viewed as m_{k+1} pixels in a small window) and has an q_k dimensional adjoint feature vector $V_{I,G(coe_j^k)}^k = (v_{j,1}^k, v_{j,2}^k, \cdots, v_{j,q_k}^k)$, $j = 1, \cdots, m_{k+1}$.

$$
\begin{aligned}
V_{I,G(coe^{k+1})}^{k+1} &= (v_1^{k+1}, v_2^{k+1}, ..., v_{2^{m_{k+1}}}^{k+1}) \\
&= \left(f_1(V_S(G(coe^{k+1}))), ..., f_{2^{m_{k+1}}}(V_S(G(coe^{k+1}))) \right)
\end{aligned}
\tag{6.2}
$$

Where $V_S(G(coe^{k+1})) = \left(V_{I,G(coe_0^k)}^k, ..., V_{I,G(coe_{m_{k+1}}^k)}^k \right)$, $V_{I,G(coe_j^k)}^k$, is the adjoint feature vector of a granule $G(coe_j^k)$ contained in $G(coe^{k+1})$, and every $f_j(X_1, ..., X_{m_{k+1}})$, $j = 1, 2, ..., 2^{m_{k+1}}$, is a fuzzy logical function of fuzzy vectors $X_1, ..., X_{m_{k+1}}$.

For example, in one dimensional case, $X_i - x_i$, $f_j(X_1, ..., X_{m_{k+1}})$ can be the jth fuzzy conjunct function of all components of fuzzy variables $x_1, x_2 ..., x_{m_{k+1}}$, i.e.

$$
f_1(X_1, \cdots, X_{m_{k+1}}) = \bar{x}_1 \wedge \bar{x}_2 \cdots \wedge \bar{x}_{m_{k+1}};
$$

$$
f_2(X_1, \cdots, X_{m_{k+1}}) = x_1 \wedge \bar{x}_2 \cdots \wedge \bar{x}_{m_{k+1}},
$$

$$
\cdot
$$

$$
\cdot
$$

$$
\cdot
$$

$$
f_{2^{m_{k+1}}}(X_1, \cdots, X_{m_{k+1}}) = x_1 \wedge x_2 \cdots \wedge x_{m_{k+1}}.
$$

In fact $f_j(X_1, ..., X_{m_{k+1}})$ tries to decide if the vectors set $(X_1, ..., X_{m_{k+1}})$ in a small window accords with the jth model. So we denote such kind $V_{I,G(coe^{k+1})}^{k+1}$ as a model fitting rate MFR.

The 2nd **step(a)** is the model frequency MF step, MF is computed as Eq. (6.3). In the case of images, it computes the matching rate of a small image block with a model in a small window.

$$V^{k+2}_{I,G(coe^{k+2})} = (v^{k+2}_1, v^{k+2}_2, ..., v^{k+2}_{2^{m_{k+2}}})$$
$$= \left(\sum_{1 \le j \le m_{k+2}} f_1(V_S(G(coe_j^{k+1}))), \cdots, \sum_{1 \le j \le m_{k+2}} f_{2^{m_{k+2}}}(V_S(G(coe_j^{k+1}))) \right) \tag{6.3}$$

Where every $f_j(X), j = 0, 1, ..., 2^{m_{k+2}} - 1$, is a fuzzy logical function.

In the 2nd **step (b)** is the histograms HIS step, a histograms should be computed in a much more large window, so Eq. (6.4) tries to compute the histogram of patterns in a much more larger granule leveled $k + 2$, which can be viewed as a set of $k + 1$ -level granules $G(coe_j^{k+1})$ with size m_{k+2}. Eq. (6.4) is similar to Eq. (6.3) except $f_j(X_1, ..., X_{m_{k+1}})$ in Eq. (6.3) is replaced by the binary function $bf_j(X_1, ..., X_{m_{k+1}}) = (f_j(X_1, ..., X_{m_{k+1}}) > thr)$.

$$bV^{k+2}_{I,G(coe^{k+2})} = (bv^{k+2}_1, bv^{k+2}_2, ..., bv^{k+2}_{2^{m_{k+2}}})$$
$$= \left(\sum_{1 \le j \le m_{k+2}} bf_1(V_S(G(coe_j^{k+1}))), \cdots, \sum_{1 \le j \le m_{k+2}} bf_{2^{m_{k+2}}}(V_S(G(coe_j^{k+1}))) \right) \tag{6.4}$$

Where bv_j^{k+2} is the frequency of $G(coe^{k+2})$'s son granules which have adjiont feature vectors according with

$$bf_j(V_S(G(coe_j^{k+1}))) = \left(f_j(V_S(G(coe_j^{k+1}))) \ge thr\right), \ thr \ge 0, j = 0, 1, 2, .., 2^{m_{k+2}} - 1.$$

An adjiont feature vector computed by Eq. (6.3) is denoted as model matching fuzzy frequency feature vector$(mmfV)$; whereas, it is denoted as histogram adjiont feature vector$(hisV)$, if it is computed by Eq. (6.4).

In the following section, we try to apply above framework in the task of image matting.

6.1.1 Perception Granular Computing for Image Matting

According to Levin A et al.(2008) [35], image matting refers to the problem of softly extracting the foreground object from an input image and a trimap image. "Tripmap" means three kinds of regions, white denotes definite foreground region, black denotes definite back ground region and gray denotes undefined region. Now we try to apply above defined framework of GDL in the task of image matting. Natural image matting is of central importance in image and video editing. Formally, image matting methods take as input an image I, which is assumed to be a composite of a foreground image F and a background image B. The color of the i-th pixel is assumed to be a linear combination of the corresponding foreground and background colors:

$$I_i = F_i \alpha_i + B_i(1 - \alpha_i) \tag{6.5}$$

where α_i is the pixels foreground opacity or alpha matte , F_i is the foreground color, and B_i is the background color [35] .

Now the problem is that when an image I is given, how can we calculate F_i, B_i and α_i? In order to calculate F_i, B_i and α_i, for the grayscale case, we make the assumption that both $F_i = F$ and $B_i = B$ are approximately constant over a small window around each pixel. Note that assuming F and B are locally smooth does not mean that the input image I is locally smooth, since discontinuities in α_i can account for the discontinuities in I. This assumption allows us to rewrite Eq. (6.5) expressing α_i as a linear function of the image I:

$$\alpha_i = a_j^T I_i + b_j, \forall i \in W_j, j = 1, ..., k_W \qquad (6.6)$$

here k_W is the number of small windows, $a_j = \frac{1}{F-B}$ and $b_j = -\frac{B}{F-B}$ if some pixels have assigned a label l_i, then according to Eq. (6.6), the cost function Eq. (6.1) can be computed as Eq. (6.7), otherwise the second item in Eq. (6.7) is zero, i.e, in this case $l_i = \alpha_i$.

$$J_k(\vec{\alpha}, a_k, b_k) = \sum_{i \in W_k} (\alpha_i - a_k^T I_i - b_k)^2 + \sum_{i \in W_k} (l_i - \alpha_i)^2 + \epsilon a_k^T a_k \qquad (6.7)$$

The parameters can be calculated by the optimization:

$$J_k = \min_{\vec{\alpha}, a, b} J_k(\vec{\alpha}, a, b)$$

here $\vec{\alpha} = (\alpha_0, \alpha_1, \cdots, \alpha_{W_k})$. According to Eq. (6.6), the labeled pixels can transmit their labels to similar near by pixels, the rule of labels' transmission can be summarized as :

For a labeled pixel: if a pixel i has already been forced a label l_i, then

$$l_i = a_j^T I_i + b_j, \forall i \in W_j. \qquad (6.8)$$

For a unlabeled pixel: according to Eq. (6.8), if an unlabeled pixel I_q has same pixel value with a labeled pixel I_i in a small window, then I_q should be assigned the same label as I_i, i.e.

$$l_q = a_j^T I_q + b_j = a_j^T I_i + b_j = I_i, \forall i \in W_j. \qquad (6.9)$$

In other words, the **labels transfer** accords with the rule: **Similar pixel must have similar label.**

When more than one pixels have been assigned labels, these labels may contradict with each other under the constraint of Eq. (6.6), in this case, Eq. (6.6) can only give out an approximate solution of linear optimization. For the whole image or all windows, the cost function is listed as:

$$J(\vec{\alpha}, a, b) = \sum_{k \in I} \left(\sum_{i \in W_k} (\alpha_i - a_k^T I_i - b_k)^2 + \epsilon a_k^T a_k \right) + \sum_{k \in I} \sum_{i \in W_k} (l_i - \alpha_i)^2 \qquad (6.10)$$

6.1.2 The Generalization of Image Matting

Above mentioned processing of image matting can be generalized in the framework of granular systems, we denote such kind granular deep learning as "GDL for image understanding ($IUGDL$)" In the framework of $IUGDL$, at first, we should extend the rule of labels transferring from pixels to small image blocks in small windows. The novel rule of labels' transferring says that similar image blocks in small windows should have similar labels.

Granular computing can be viewed as a technique of fenestration. In a larger granule $G(coe^{l+2})$, similar to α_i and b_i in Eq. (6.6), we suppose the label's vector $L_{G(coe^{l+1})}$ and $B_{G(coe^{l+2})}$ accord with

$$L_{G(coe^{l+1})} = \mathbb{A}_{G(coe^{l+1})}{}^T \cdot F(V^{l+1}_{I,G(coe^{l+1})}, \mathbb{W}) + B_{G(coe^{l+2})}, \forall G(coe^{l+1}) \in G(coe^{l+2}) \tag{6.11}$$

Where $V^{l+1}_{I,G(coe^{l+1})}$ can be $V^{k+1}_{I,G(coe^{k+1})}$ in Eq. (6.2), and $F(\cdot, \mathbb{W}))$ with a parameter matrix $\mathbb{W}$ is a function, which changes an adjoint feature vector to a label vector.

In the task of image matting, the label vector $L_{G(coe^{l+1})}$ is just a scale value $\alpha_{G(coe^{l+1})}$, in this case, $F(\cdot, \mathbb{W})$ can be a fuzzy logical function.

If above mentioned histogram is used, labels should be assigned to level $l + 2$ granules in the task of labels' extension.

$$L_{G(coe^{l+2})} = \mathbb{A}_{G(coe^{l+3})}{}^T \cdot F(bV^{l+2}_{I,G(coe^{l+2})}, \mathbb{W}) + B_{G(coe^{l+3})}, \forall G(coe^{l+2}) \in G(coe^{l+3}) \tag{6.12}$$

Where $F(\cdot)$ is a function which changes the adjoint feature vector $bV^{l+2}_{I,G(coe^{l+2})}$ to a label vector, and $bV^{l+2}_{I,G(coe^{l+2})}$ is $bV^{k+2}_{I,G(coe^{k+2})}$ in Eq. (6.4).

The cost or risk function for Eq. (6.11) is listed as:

$$J(L, \mathbb{A}, B, \mathbb{W}) = \sum_{C_{G(coe^{l+2})} \in Grid_{l+2}} R(G(coe^{l+2})) + \sum_{C_{G(coe^{l+2})} \in Grid_{l+2}} L_{err}(G(coe^{l+2})) + \epsilon \parallel \mathbb{A}_{G(coe^{l+2})} \parallel \cdot \tag{6.13}$$

here $C_{G(coe^{l+2})}$ is the centers set of the granule $G(coe^{l+2})$, $Grid_{l+2}$ is the level $l + 2$ centers grid upon an image I, $R(G(coe^{l+2}))$ (Eq. (6.14)) is the cost or risk for the granule $G(coe^{l+2})$ and $L_{err}(G(coe^{l+2}))$ is the error for the labels estimating in $G(coe^{l+2})$(Eq. (6.15)),$\parallel \mathbb{A}_{G(coe^{l+2})} \parallel$ is the regular item.

$$R(G(coe^{l+2})) = \sum_{G(coe^{l+1}) \in G(coe^{l+2})} \parallel L_{G(coe^{l+1})} - \mathbb{A}_{G(coe^{l+2})}{}^T F(V^{l+1}_{I,G(coe^{l+1})}, \mathbb{W}) - B_{G(coe^{l+2})} \parallel^{2} \cdot \tag{6.14}$$

$$L_{err}(G(coe^{l+2})) = \sum_{G(coe^{l+1}) \in \mathbf{S} \subseteq G(coe^{l+2})} (T_{G(coe^{l+1})} - L_{G(coe^{l+1})})^{2} \cdot \tag{6.15}$$

Here $T_{G(coe^{l+1})}$ is the target of the label vector $L_{G(coe^{l+1})}$, $\mathbf{S}$ is a subset of level $l + 1$ granules in $G(coe^{l+2})$, and all granules in $\mathbf{S}$ are artificially labeled.

Similarly, for binary histogram, the cost function for Eq. (6.12) can be achieved by adding one level the level $l + 2$ in Eq.(6.13) and (6.14), (6.15), i.e. replacing $V^{l+1}_{I,G(coe^{l+1})}$ with $bV^{l+2}_{I,G(coe^{l+2})}$ in a large father granule $G(coe^{l+3})$.

Define $\mathbb{A}_{G(coe^{l+1})}{}^T \cdot F(V^{l+1}_{I,G(coe^{l+1})}, \mathbb{W}) + B_{G(coe^{l+2})}$ as $F_L(V^{l+1}_{I,G(coe^{l+1})}, \mathbb{W})$, according to the universal approximate theorem [24], $F_L(V_{I,G(coe^{l+1})}^{l+1}, \mathbb{W})$ can be computed by a 2 layers' neural network as:

$$F_L(V_{I,G(coe^{l+1})}^{l+1}, \mathbb{W}) = \mathbb{W}_{out} \cdot F_H(V_{I,G(coe^{l+1})}^{l+1}, \mathbb{W}_{hidden}) \tag{6.16}$$

here the layered mapping $F_H(V_{I,G(coe^{l+1})}^{l+1})$ is a nonlinear mapping from $R^{q_{l+1}}$ to R^{m_H}, m_H is the number of the last hidden layer's neurons. $\mathbb{W}_{out}$ can be computed by PSVM, which tries to minimize Eq.(6.17).

$$\min_{\mathbb{W}_{out}} R(\mathbb{W}_{out}) = \sum_{G(coe^{l+1}) \in \mathbf{S}} (T_{G(coe^{l+1})} - F_L(V_{I,G(coe^{l+1})}^{l+1}, \mathbb{W} = \mathbb{W}_{out} \cup \mathbb{W}_{hidden}))^2. \tag{6.17}$$

If $F_L(V_{I,G(coe^{l+1})}^{l+1}, \mathbb{W} = \mathbb{W}_{out} \cup \mathbb{W}_{hidden})$ is a three layers' neural network, based on the theorem proposed by S. Tamura et al. (1997)([57]), the parameters $\mathbb{W}_{hidden}$ in the first nonlinear layer $F_H(V_{I,G(coe^{l+1})}^{l+1})$ can be arbitrary set.

Not loosing generality, we suppose the label vector $L_{G(coe^{l+1})}$ of $G(coe^{l+1})$ is a scalar $l_{G(coe^{l+1})}$. In this case, similar to [35], computing $\mathbb{A}$ and B can be translated to compute L in Eq.(6.18).

$$\sum_{C_{G(coe^{l+2})} \in Grid_{l+2}} R(G(coe^{l+2})) = L^T \cdot \mathbb{P} \cdot L \tag{6.18}$$

Here $L = (l_{G(coe_1^{(l+1)})}, l_{G(coe_2^{(l+1)})}, \cdots, l_{G(coe_n^{(l+1)})})^T$ and all $G(coe_j^{(l+1)}) \in C_{ov}^{l+1}(I), j = 1, \cdots, n$, $C_{ov}^{l+1}(I)$ is the level $l+1$ cover of the image I; $\mathbb{P}$ is a $n \times n$ sparse matrix, n is the size of $C_{ov}^{l+1}(I)$, every element $\mathbb{P}(i,j)$ in $\mathbb{P}$ corresponding to a couple of level $l+1$ granules $G(coe_i^{(l+1)})$ and $G(coe_j^{(l+1)})$. If $G(coe_i^{(l+1)})$ and $G(coe_j^{(l+1)})$ do not belong to any level $l+2$ granules at same time, $\mathbb{P}(i,j) = 0$; otherwise, $\mathbb{P}(i,j)$ can be computed in a way similar to [35], i.e. can be computed as below

$$\mathbb{P}(i,j) = \sum_{G(coe^{l+2}) \in C_{ov}^{l+2}(I)|G(coe_i^{l+1}),G(coe_j^{l+1}) \in G(coe^{l+2})} \{\delta_{ij} - \frac{1}{|G(coe^{l+2})|}[1 + \eta \cdot F_{-\mu,i}^T \cdot F_{-\mu,j}]\}$$
$$F_{-\mu,i} = F(V_{I,G(coe_i^{l+1})}^{l+1}, \mathbb{W}) - \mu_{G(coe^{l+2})} \text{ and } F_{-\mu,j} = F(V_{I,G(coe_j^{l+1})}^{l+1}, \mathbb{W}) - \mu_{G(coe^{l+2})}; \tag{6.19}$$

here $F(V_{I,G(coe_i^{l+1})}, \mathbb{W})$ is a scale, $G(coe_i^{l+2})$ can be viewed as a window of $G(coe_i^{l+1})$, $\eta = \frac{1}{\frac{\epsilon}{|G(coe^{l+2})|} + \sigma_{G(coe^{l+2})}}$, $\mu_{G(coe^{l+2})}$ and $\sigma_{G(coe^{l+2})}$ are the corresponding mean and variance of the $F(V_{I,G(coe_i^{l+1})}, \mathbb{W})$ in $G(coe_i^{l+2})$, $C_{ov}^{l+2}(I)$ is the level $l+2$ cover of the whole image I, $|G(coe^{l+2})|$ is the number of all level $l+1$ granules $G(coe^{l+1})$ contained in $G(coe^{l+2})$.

If we solve the equation $J(L)$ directly, the trivial result will be get as $L = 0$. Clearly that's not what we want, so we need more information from user constrain. For instances, we need user to scribble few definitely foreground pixels and background pixels that can be organized as a vector denoted as $T_{G(coe^{(l+1)})}$, which is denoted as "**trimaps**". Simply, we give value 1 to foreground pixels and 0 to background pixels. Then a new object function formed:

$$E(L) =$$
$$L^T \cdot \mathbb{P} \cdot L + \lambda(L - T)^T \cdot \mathbb{D} \cdot (L - T) \tag{6.20}$$

where $\mathbb{D}$ is the identity matrix.

To minima this object function, we need solve the equation:

$$(\mathbb{P} + \lambda\mathbb{D}) \cdot L = \lambda\mathbb{D} \cdot T \tag{6.21}$$

Eq.(6.21) can be solved as:

$$L = (\mathbb{P} + \lambda\mathbb{D})^{-1} \cdot \lambda\mathbb{D} \cdot T \tag{6.22}$$

Form the layered granular deep learning point of view, the fact $\mathbb{P}(i,j) \neq 0$ means that two level $l + 1$ granules $G(coe_i^{(l+1)})$ and $G(coe_j^{(l+1)})$ belong to at least one level $l+2$ granule $G(coe^{(l+2)})$, so $\mathbb{P}(i,j)$ contains the information about similarity and neighborhood of $G(coe_i^{(l+1)})$ and $G(coe_j^{(l+1)})$. In this case, $\mathbb{P}(i,j)$ can be viewed as a dimension of the adjoint feature vector of $G(coe^{(l+2)})$. The label vector $L = (L_{G(coe_1^{(l+1)})}, L_{G(coe_2^{(l+1)})}, \cdots, L_{G(coe_n^{(l+1)})})^T$ is a vector for all level $l + 1$ granules which can be viewed as an adjoint feature vector of a large level $l + 3$ granule $G(coe^{(l+3)})$ which contains all level $l + 2$ granules.

Unfortunately if the separating of foreground and background is based on color not texture, above approach has no benefit. In order to overcome this shortness, we modify Eq.(6.11) into Eq.(6.23).

$$L_{G(coe^{l+1})} = \mathbb{A}_{G(coe^{l+1})}^{T} \cdot F_{hybrid}(V_{I,G(coe^{l+1})}^{l+1}, \mathbb{W}) + B_{G(coe^{l+2})}, \forall G(coe^{l+1}) \in G(coe^{l+2}) \tag{6.23}$$

Where $F_{hybrid}(V_{I,G(coe^{l+1})}^{l+1}, \mathbb{W})$ is defined as .

$$F_{hybrid}(V_{I,G(coe^{l+1})}^{l+1}, \mathbb{W}) = \gamma \cdot F_L(V_{I,G(coe^{l+1})}^{l+1}, \mathbb{W}) + (1 - \gamma) \cdot I \tag{6.24}$$

where $F_L(V_{I,G(coe^{l+1})}^{l+1}, \mathbb{W})$ is computed by minimizing Eq. (6.17), and I can be viewed as an output of an auto encoder in deep learning [5].

Chapter 7

Perception Granular System for the Image Matting Task

7.1 Perception Granular System for the Image Matting Task

In this section, we try to design a Perception Granular system of Columnar Organization($COGsys$) for the image matting task, here only nested layered GDL is needed. For the image matting task, the fuzzy label of foreground or background is described by the parameter α. For the task of image matting, we take color or texture in local window as our input feature, and the trimap image as the target. After training, the fuzzy logical granular deep learning will generate the result of alpha matte. In the application of alpha matting, the recognition of our Leveled Granular System (see Fig. 7.1) is started with the recognition orientation or simple structure of local patterns by the function $f_j(V_S(G(coe^k)))$ in Eq. (6.3) or (6.4), then the trimap image (every pixel of a trimap image is just a label vector) is computed based on these local patterns by Eq. (6.22).

Layered neural network described by Eq. (7.1) is used to design GDL. The weight w_i in Eq. (7.1) can be viewed as connections among granules. A nested layered GDL is defined by the input and output relation of a granular deep learning on a granular system. Just as above mentioned, there are three ways to design weights of a layered GDL:according to the binary or fuzzy logical relation about this layered GDL and according to the input and output relation function $f_i(x_1, x_2, x_3, \ldots, x_n)$ from training samples.

$$U_{l+1,i} = \sum_k w_{l+1,i,k} \cdot I_{l+1,k,i}$$
$$O_{l+1,i} = S(U_{l+1,i}, T_{l+1,i}, \lambda) \tag{7.1}$$

where $S()$ is a sigmoid function showed in Eq. (7.2), and $O_{l+1,i}$ is the output of a level $l + 1$ granule.

$$S(x, t, \lambda) = 1/\{1 + exp\{-\lambda \cdot (x - t)\}\} \tag{7.2}$$

The theorem 2 guarantees that above defined granule computing can simulate a boolean function with arbitrary

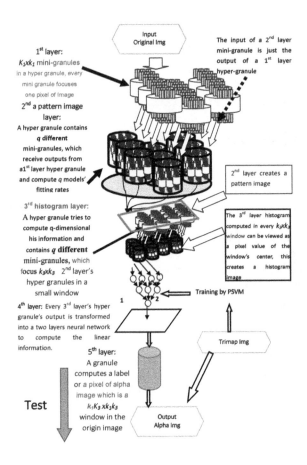

1st layer:
$K_1 x k_1$ mini-granules
in a hyper granule, every mini granule focuses one pixel of Image

2nd a pattern image layer:
A hyper granule contains *q different* mini-granules, which receive outputs from a 1st layer hyper granule and compute *q* models' fitting rates

3rd histogram layer:
A hyper granule tries to compute q-dimensional his information and contains *q different* mini-granules, which focus $k_3 x k_3$ 2nd layer's hyper granules in a small window

4th layer: Every 3rd layer's hyper granule's output is transformed into a two layers neural network to compute the linear information.

5th layer:
A granule computes a label or a pixel of alpha image which is a $k_1 K_3 x k_1 k_3$ window in the origin image

Test

Input Original Img

The input of a 2nd layer mini-granule is just the output of a 1st layer hyper-granule

2nd layer creates a pattern image

The 3rd layer histogram computed in every $k_3 x k_3$ window can be viewed as a pixel value of the window's center, this creates a histogram image

Training by PSVM

Trimap Img

Output Alpha Img

Figure 7.1: The framework of a Gsys for the task of image background and for ground separating. The output alpha image is computed by four layers' granules.

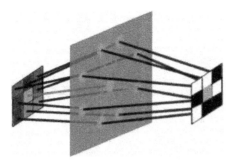

Figure 7.2: Every 1st layer granule tries to change a local image into a binary texture pattern. For a hyper granule is defined by a distance function $dis(x,c) < 3$, which is just a 3×3 small window, a hyper-granule in the 1st layer contains 9 granules, and every granule focuses only one pixel.

small error. The designing of a $Gsys$ contains two parts: (1) convex regions, (2)adjoint fuzzy logical functions for GDL.

The convex regions in the following $Gsys$ for image matting task are very simple convex regions and can be described by distance function. The input space is just an image, which is a 5-dimensional space $X = \{(x,y,r,g,b)\}$, here every example (x,y,r,g,b) represents a pixel of this image, (x,y) is the pixel's location and (r,g,b) is the pixel's color value. A nested granular system is built upon images, with fuzzy logical formula $sp(\alpha, c | dis, d, W_\omega)$ here $W_\omega = (1,1,0,0,0)$, and $d = 0$ for level 1 GDL , and $d > 1$ for higher level $GDLs$. All levels'centers are located on the whole image plane, so a level l centers' grid is just the image plane and granules are overlapped.

If there are k levels in our Gsys, the first level receives the input image I, and a kth level granule outputs the result of matting task. The relation between input and output of a level-l granule is described by Eq. (7.1). The weights among granules are designed by LPSVM, i.e. the weights of 1st and 2nd layers are designed by fuzzy logic, and the weights of the 3rd layer are designed by PSVM to learn the trimap image.

Fig.7.1 is the framework of a Gsys for the task of image background and for ground separating. The GDL of COGsys is formally defined as bellow:

7.1.1 The 1st layer– fuzzy logical layer

Every hyper-granule(Fig. 7.2) in the 1st layer tries to change a $k_1 \times k_1 = (2k+1) \times (2k+1)$ pixels' image block $I_{b(2k+1) \times (2k+1)}$ into a binary $(2k+1) \times (2k+1)$ pixels'texture pattern. The input image is normalized. A hyper-granule $HG = (g, S_F)$ in the 1st layer contains $(2k+1) \times (2k+1)$ mini-granules to focus a $(2k+1) \times (2k+1)$ small window, every mini-granule focuses only one pixel, so the convex region of a mini-granule is described by $dis(x,c) \leq 0$. A hyper-granule completes the task of image processing. There are three kinds fuzzy logical functions in a hyper-granule's S_F:

1. In a local image pattern recognition way(LIPW): the 1st processing directly transforms every pixel's value to

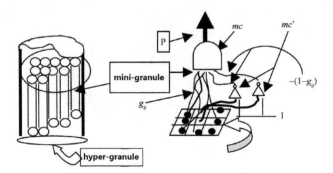

Figure 7.3: A hyper-granule in the 2nd layer contains q granules which have same receptive field and try to recognize q definite small shapes. A *'and'* granule is needed for every 2nd layer granule.

a fuzzy logical one by a sigmoid function.

$$F_1(\{I_b\}_{(2k+1)\times(2k+1)}) = \{S(p_{i,j})\}_{(2k+1)\times(2k+1)} \tag{7.3}$$

here $p_{i,j}, i,j = 1,2,\cdots,(2k+1)$ is the RGB pixel value in a small 3×3 window;

2. In a local Binary Pattern operator simulating way(LBPW). The 2nd processing is also completed by a sigmoid function; the difference is that every boundary pixel's value is fuzzy exclusive OR $\oplus$ with the center pixel's value before sending it to a sigmoid function,

$$F_2(\{I_b\}_{(2k+1)\times(2k+1)}) = \{f(p_{i,j})\}_{(2k+1)\times(2k+1)} \tag{7.4}$$

Here $f(p_{i,j}) = S(p_{i,j}\oplus p_{k+1,k+1})$ when $i,j \neq k+1$, and $f(p_{k+1,k+1}) = 0$. F_2 is similar to a Local Binary Pattern operator(LBP) mentioned in [49] as a mean of summarizing local gray-level structure. [49] was originally defined for neighborhoods, giving 8 bit codes based on the 8 pixels around the central one. The operator takes a local neighborhood around each pixel, thresholds the pixels of the neighborhood at the value of the central pixel and uses the resulting binary-valued image patch as a local image descriptor.

Such processing emphasizes the contrast of texture, and our experiments support this fact.

3. Hybrid LIPW and LBPW (LBIPW). The adjoint function $F_3(\cdot)$ in LBIPW is same as $F_2(\cdot)$ in LBPW, except that $f(p_{k+1,k+1}) = p_{k+1,k+1}$ in $F_3(\cdot)$,while $f(p_{k+1,k+1}) = 0$ in $F_2(\cdot)$.

Every granule of 1st layer has only one input weight w_{ij} in Fig. 7.2, which equals 1; when $\lambda \to +\infty$, the coefficient λ in Eq. (7.1) changes the outputs from fuzzy values to binary numbers.

wm_l

Figure 7.4: Every the 2nd layer's granule contains q granules which correspond to q modules in above picture.

7.1.2 The 2nd Pattern Matching Layer to Create a pattern Image

Every 2nd layer mini-granules try to recognize a definite shape(see Fig. 7.3) and compute $f_i(V_S(G(coe_j^{k+2})))$ or $bf_i(V_S(G(coe_j^{k+2})))$ in Eq. (6.3) or (6.4), so they share the same convex region with a 1st layer hyper-granule, which focuses on the same small $(2k+1) \times (2k+1)$ window in an image, and can be described by $dis(x,c) < 2k$. If there are total q local small patterns, a hyper-granule in the 2nd layer contains q mini-granules of the 2nd layer, which have same receptive field, but with a different adjoint fuzzy logical function, which tries to recognize a definite shape from the output of a 1st layer hyper-granule.

For example, the "∩" shape in Fig.7.3 can be described by a adjoint fuzzy logical formula (Eq.(7.5)). The "and" operator for 9 inputs in Eq.(7.5)can be created by a granule mc (see Fig.7.3). In Eq.(7.5), every pixel P_{ij} has two states m_{ij} and $\overline{m_{ij}}$. Suppose the unified gray value(or RGB value) of P_{ij} is g_{ij}, and an image module needs a high value g_{ij} at the place of m_{ij} and a low value at $\overline{m_{ij}}$. So the input for the granule mc at m_{ij} is $I_{ij} = g_{ij}$, and at $\overline{m_{ij}}$ is $I_{ij} = -(1.0 - g_{ij})$. A not gate mc' is needed for $I_{ij} = -(1.0 - g_{ij})$, here $g_{ij}, i, j = 1, 2, 3$ is the output of a 1_{st} layer hyper-granule.

$$P = m_{11} \wedge m_{12} \wedge m_{13} \wedge m_{21} \wedge m_{23} \wedge m_{31} \wedge m_{33} \wedge \overline{m}_{22} \wedge \overline{m}_{32} \tag{7.5}$$

$$w_{ij} = \begin{cases} w & \text{, if the } i,j\text{th bit of a binary pattern } = 1 \\ -w & \text{, if the } i,j\text{th bit of a binary pattern } = -1 \end{cases} \tag{7.6}$$

where for LIPW and LBIPW, $i, j = 1, 2, 3, .., (2k+1)$; for LBPW, the center 1st-layer granule is useless, so $(i = k+1, j = k+1)$ is not included. There are three kinds hyper-granules in the 2nd-layer, which receive three different outputs of a 1st-layer's hyper-granule, so a hyper-granule in the 2nd-layer may work in one of following three ways:

1. In the local image pattern recognition way(LIPW): every 2nd layer hyper-granule contains q 2nd-layer's mini-granules, and inputs of these 2nd-layer's mini-granules come from a 1st-layer's hyper-granule which works in LIPW way. Every 2nd-layer's hyper-granule tries to classify the image block in this window into q binary texture patterns(BTP), e.g. eight important BTPs are shown in Fig. 7.4. The pixel value is "1" for white and "-1" for black. In this mode, $2k+1 \times 2k+1$ granules of the 1st layer output a $2k+1 \times 2k+1$ vector, i.e., a $2k+1 \times 2k+1$ fuzzy logical pattern of a BTP, which is computed by a sigmoid function.

2. In the local Binary Pattern operator simulating way(LBPW), a 2nd-layer's hyper-granule contains q 2nd-layer's mini-granules which receive input from the output of a 1st-layer's hyper-granule, which works in the way of LBPW.

Page 61

3. In the hybrid LIPW and LBPW (LBIPW)way, a 2nd-layer's hyper-granule contains q 2nd-layer's mini-granules which receive input from the output of a 1st-layer's hyper-granule, which has $(2k+1) \times (2k+1)$-dimensions.

In our system, a $Gsys$ is built for every color channel R,G or B, so a hyper-granule in the 2nd layer has a $q \times 3$ dimensions output. All hyper-granules in the 2nd layer create a pattern image.

As a binary logical layer, in order to recognize a binary pattern, a fuzzy 'and' granule with index i is needed (see Fig. 7.3)for every 2nd-layer granule, and the weights of this 'and' granule to the 1st-layer granules are set as Eq (7.6), the corresponding parameters in Eq. (7.1) are set as the threshold is set according to the fuzzy degree. Usually, $t_i = 5.1$, and $\lambda = 0.9$.

7.1.3 The 3rd layer–To Compute Histogram Image

A hyper granule in the 3rd layer contains q different mini-granules, which focus $k_3 \times k_3$ 2nd layers hyper granules in a small window, tries to compute q-dimensional histogram of information by summing the output of these 2nd layers hyper granules.

7.1.4 The 4th layer–Linear Information of Labels $F(V^{l+1}_{I,G(coe^{l+1})}, \mathbb{W})$

Every 3rd layers hyper granules output is transformed into a two layers neural network, which is trained by PSVM to compute the linear information of labels $F(V^{l+1}_{I,G(coe^{l+1})}, \mathbb{W})$ in Eq.(6.11) or Eq.(6.12). This layered neural network is trained to make the L_{err} in Eq.(6.15) smallest.

7.1.5 The 5th layer–the layer for computing label vector L

In this layer, the Lapidarian matrix $\mathbb{P}(i,j)$, which contains the information about similarity and neighborhood of $G(coe^{(3)}_i)$ and $G(coe^{(3)}_j)$, is computed by Eq.(6.19) at first. After that, the label vectors $L = (l_{G(coe^{(3)}_1)}, l_{G(coe^{(3)}_2)}, \cdots, l_{G(coe^{(3)}_n)})^T$ is computed, here every label $l_{G(coe^{(3)}_i)}$ is a label of a smaller image block with size $k_1 k_3 \times k_1 k_3$ in the original image.

Two concrete applications:

(1).Background and Foreground Separating: In this layer, the Lapidarian matrix $\mathbb{P}(i,j)$, which contains the information about similarity and neighborhood of $G(coe^{(3)}_i)$ and $G(coe^{(3)}_j)$, is computed by Eq.(6.19) at first. After that, the label vectors $L = (l_{G(coe^{(3)}_1)}, l_{G(coe^{(3)}_2)}, \cdots, l_{G(coe^{(3)}_n)})^T$ is computed, here every label $l_{G(coe^{(3)}_i)}$ is a label of a smaller image block with size $k_1 k_3 \times k_1 k_3$ in the original image.

In the application of background and foreground separating, the 1st fuzzy logical layer is not important, there are eight types of the level 2nd hyper-granules, which complete the task of local pattern matching in LIPW way for gray images or LBPW for color images. At the 2nd layer of Fig.7.1, a hyper granule contains 256 3×3 mini-granules and compute fitting rates (MFR) about a small image block. These mini-granules cover whole image except for surround pixels of the image. At the 3rd layer of Fig.7.1, there are 256 different types of hyper granules, each of them focuses 34×34 hyper-granules in the 2nd layer, and computes a 3×256 dimensional vector, which is delivered to the 4th layer- a set of two layered neural networks. These layered neural networks compute linear information of labels $F(V^{l+1}_{I,G(coe^{l+1})}, \mathbb{W})$ by Eq.(6.17). In the 5th layer of Fig.7.1, the output alpha image is computed by Eq.(6.22), here every pixel of the alpha image is just a fuzzy label(1:object,0:background) of a smaller image brock with size 9×9 . *(2).Background and Foreground Separating in Haze-free task*:

Haze-free task is a special case of image matting. The texture of haze is fixed, texture recognition is no useful for a haze free task, so the level 3 is omitted. The level 4 and 5 are listed as bellow:

The 4th layer–alogical layer for haze-free

The convex region of the 2nd layer can also be described by $dis(x,c) < 2$. The output of a hyper-granule in the 2nd layer, which has 3×256 or 3×512 dimensions, is transformed to the 4th-layer granules, which is a 2 layers neural network, to compute the similarity parameter or fuzzy value α_i in Eq. (6.4), the weights of this layer is computed by psvm, the target is provided by so called dark channel prior which is computed by the approach mentioned in [25]. As all α_i are optimised on the whole image, in this layer,the whole image is the only convex region. As the small windows focused by hyper-granules in the 2nd-layer are overlapped, the focuses of 4th-layer's granules are also overlapped.

The 5th layer–fuzzy logical layer for haze free

In this layer, a granule tries to remove the haze from original image. A granule in the 5th layer computes a pixel of a haze free image according to fuzzy logical equation Eq. (7.7)

$$
\begin{aligned}
I_i(x) &= \min\{q, \alpha_i(x) \cdot J_i(x) + (1 - \alpha_i(x)) \cdot A_i\} \\
&= J_i(x) \oplus_f A_i
\end{aligned}
\tag{7.7}
$$

where J_i is the haze free image, I_i is the original image, A_i is the global atmospheric light which can be estimated from dark channel prior, α_i is the alpha matte generated by 4th layer, and $\oplus_f$ is the q-value Weighted Bounded sum with weights $w_1 = \alpha_i(x)$, $w_2 = 1 - \alpha_i(x)$, here q is max gray or RGB value of a pixel, and $\alpha_i(x)$ and $(1 - \alpha_i(x))$ are weights. Although we can use back propagation approach to compute pixels' value $J_i(x)$ given the haze image pixel value $I_i(x)$ based on Eq. (7.7), for the sake of simplicity, we directly use the Eq. (7.8) mentioned by [25] to compute the haze free image. As every $\alpha_i(x)$ is computed upon the whole image, the pixel of haze-free image is also computed upon whole image, so the whole image is also the convex region of this layer.

$$
J_i(x) = \frac{I_i(x) - A_i}{max(\alpha_i(x), \alpha_0)} + A_i
\tag{7.8}
$$

where J_i is the haze free image, I_i is the original image, A_i is the global atmospheric light which can be estimated from dark channel prior, α_i is the alpha matte generated by 3rd layer, and α_0 is a threshold, a typical value is 1.

7.2 Experiments result

Now we list two experiments about image matting.

1. Foreground and background separation

   In Fig.7.5, the 1st row is the origin images, the 2nd row is the trimaps, the white part and black part in a trimap are foreground and back ground scrabbled by us, the gray part is the unknown part, its pixels'labels should

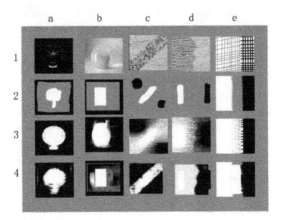

Figure 7.5: In column a, old approach in [35] and our novel granular matting approach have similar ability to separate the fore and back ground; in the column b, the difference of foreground background lies in gray level not texture, our novel granular matting approach fails to separating foreground and background. In c, d, e, we can see that our novel granular matting approach is more powerful than the old approach to recognize textures.

be computed by our matting approach. The 3rd row is the results computed by approach described in [35], i.e. in Eq.(6.24) $\gamma = 0$, and the 4th row the result computed by our novel granular matting approach, i.e. in Eq.(6.24) $\gamma = 1$. Form Fig.7.5, we can see that our novel granular matting approach is more powerful than the old approach in [35]to recognize textures. In collum b of Fig.7.5, the difference of foreground background lies in gray level not texture, our novel granular matting approach fails to separating foreground and background. So multi scale granular computing is a sound approach for back ground and foreground separating based on texture difference.

2. The Haze-Free and texture information entropy

Texture information can give out a rough measure about the effect of haze-freeing, we use the entropy of the texture histogram to measure the effect of deleting haze from images. The entropy of the histogram is described in Eq. (7.9).

Haze makes the texture of an image unclear, so theoretically speaking, haze removing will increase the entropy of the texture histogram.

$$Entropy : H = - \sum_{i=0}^{G-1} p(i) log_2[p(i)] \tag{7.9}$$

The $p(i)$ denote the rate of each pattern in histogram. In general $p(i)$ define in Eq. (7.10), for an image with width N and hight M. Here patterns we use are the LBPs in Eq. (7.4), where $S(i_n - i_C) = 1$, if $i_n > i_C + 10$ else $S(i_n - i_C) = 0$.

$$p(i) = h(i)/(NM), i = 0, 1, \ldots, G - 1 \qquad (7.10)$$

In Fig. 7.6, (a),(b),(c),(d) and (e) are the results of LBPW, LBIPW, LIPW, the linear mode (LMKH) by [25], and the original image respectively. From Fig. 7.6, we can see that the texture structure in the waist of a mountain becomes vaguer from LBPW, LBIPW, LIPW to LMKH. For the sake of the 2nd kind processing in the 1st-layer's granules pays much more attention to the contrast, LBPW has the highest ability to remove the haze, LBPW and LIPW are complementary approaches, LBIPW, which is the cooperation of them, has a similar ability as the linear approach proposed by [25].

According to the results showed in the Table. 7.1, which are about texture information entropy of the image, we can see that the texture information entropy is increased after haze-free processing, so our approaches have higher ability to increase the texture information entropy than the linear approach proposed by [25]. Theoretically speaking, LBPW is a pure texture processing, so LBPW has a highest value, LIPW is much more weaker than LBPW, LBIPW is the hybrid of LBPW and LIPW, so it has a average ability. The texture information entropy of the Area1 correctly reflects this fact. But for the Area2, as it already has a clearest texture structure in the original image, the deleting of haze may cause overdone. The texture information is over emphasized by LBPW in the Aera2, so it has a lowest texture information entropy and almost becomes a dark area. This fact means that overtreatment is more easier to appear in a non linear processing than a linear one in the haze-free task.

3. The effect about the degree of fuzzyness

Just as the theorem 1 mentioned above, the parameter λ in Eq. (7.2) can control the fuzzyness of a granule, when the parameter λ in Eq. (7.2) tends to infinite, a granule behaves from a fuzzy logical formula to a binary logical formula. This experiment is about the relation among the precision($rmse$) of PSVM learning and λ parameters in the first and second layer. LBPW is a pure texture processing and pays much more attention to the contrast of an image's nearby pixels, a set of large λ is necessary for a low $rmse$, which corresponds to binary logic; but LBIPW and LIPW aphe pear to prefer fuzzy logic for a set of small λ when $rmse$ is small. A possible explanation for this fact is that LBP proposed by T. Ojala et al.(1996) [49] is binary, not fuzzy, and has a sound classification ability for image understanding under binary pattern, but LBIPW and LIPW are not binary, they have fuzzy information at least for the center pixel of a 3×3 small window.(Fig. 7.7)

4. The comparison between our approach and LMKH

To illustrate the effect of our approach in haze-free task, we apply it on the other images and compare with LMKH (Fig. 7.8). Half of the result is better than the LMKH, the rest is as good as the LMKH by manual

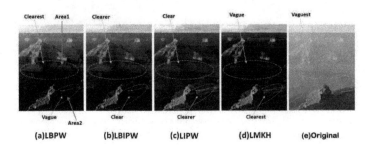

(a)LBPW   (b)LBIPW   (c)LIPW   (d)LMKH   (e)Original

Figure 7.6: The Processing Result of Granular System for Visual Haze-Free Task

Area	LBPW	LBIPW	LIPW	LMKH	Original
Area1	5.4852	5.2906	5.1593	4.8323	1.0893
Area2	6.1091	10.3280	10.2999	9.1759	8.3718

Table 7.1: The texture information entropy of the image blocks (Area1:the waist of a mountain; Area2:right bottom corner)in the Fig. 7.6

evaluation.

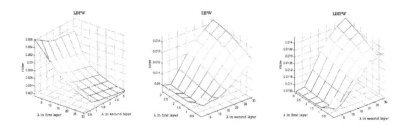

Figure 7.7: The relation among the precision($rmse$) of PSVM learning and λ parameters in the first and second layer, the parameter λ inEq. (7.2) can control the fuzzyness of a granule.

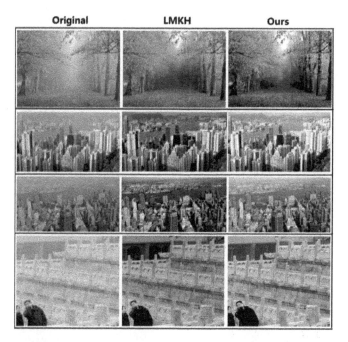

Figure 7.8: More result of Granular System for Visual Haze-Free Task.

Chapter 8

Discussion

In this book, we probe the possibility of abstracting the complicate processing of visual perception to a simply described computing model, the answer is "yes". We give out a concrete example to show that the theory of GrC can help us to design the brain-like computer. The concept of granular computing is proposed by Zadeh[1]. Just as he said: a granule is a clump of objects (points) drawn together by indistinguishability, similarity, proximity or functionality. The necessary of granular computing to study the information transformation in the pattern recognition lies in indistinguishability, similarity, proximity or functionality of sensed information. Due to the local similarity in the information processing of pattern recognition, multi-scale information processing is a common phenomenon in pattern recognition. Theoretical analysis promises that the GrC based on fuzzy logical inference and the leveled multi scale granular system described by fuzzy logical formulae can simulate all multi-scale information processing with arbitrary small error. Here the word "leveled" means no recurrent computing is not applied in GrC. For GrC, recurrent computing is used in the procession of parameters learning. These facts are very important for the hot approach-deep learning.

In this book, we use a novel designing approach(LPSVM) to design a granular system similar to the structure of columnar organization of visual cortex, We demonstrate that fuzzy logic and machine learning can be hybrid and cooperated easily to design a granular system. The experimental results show that LPSVM is a promising approach for designing of a leveled granular system similar to a columnar organization for image-matting task.

This approach not only give out a novel concrete realization of abstract models for granular computing mentioned Lin T Y.(2012) [43], but also gives a new focus for deep learning. For more,the corresponding of GrC can simulate multi-scale information processing for the task of haze-free of images, and our experiments show that our approach has some approvement for the task of haze-free comparing to the approach proposed by the linear approach proposed by [25].

Although our LPSVM gives out a concrete example for designing a granular system of image matting, many details of LPSVM should be studied in pattern recognition under the framework of deep learning, especially for the layered feature abstraction in pattern recognition. We will further expand the investigation by looking at other nested layered computing for more complex tasks. For feedback is important for many visual tasks in dynamical situations, we have also augmented our layered granular computing to a more general one which allows for both feedback and dynamical regulation for computer vision. Much more research will need to be done in future.

Acknowledgments

This work is partially supported by the National Program on Key Basic Research Project (973 Program) (No. 2013CB329502),
the National Natural Science Foundation of China (No. 61072085,61035003)

Bibliography

[1] HDI Abarbanel, Mikhail Izrailevich Rabinovich, A Selverston, MV Bazhenov, R Huerta, MM Sushchik, and LL Rubchinskii. Synchronisation in neural networks. *Physics-Uspekhi*, 39(4):337–362, 1996.

[2] Jonathan S Bakin, Ken Nakayama, and Charles D Gilbert. Visual responses in monkey areas v1 and v2 to three-dimensional surface configurations. *The Journal of Neuroscience*, 20(21):8188–8198, 2000.

[3] Andrzej Bargiela and Witold Pedrycz. The roots of granular computing. In *GrC*, pages 806–809, 2006.

[4] Horace B Barlow, Colin Blakemore, and John D Pettigrew. The neural mechanism of binocular depth discrimination. *The Journal of physiology*, 193(2):327, 1967.

[5] Yoshua Bengio. Learning deep architectures for ai. *Foundations and trends® in Machine Learning*, 2(1):1–127, 2009.

[6] Frank Buchholtz, Jorge Golowasch, IRVING R Epstein, and Eve Marder. Mathematical model of an identified stomatogastric ganglion neuron. *Journal of neurophysiology*, 67(2):332–340, 1992.

[7] AN Burkitt. A review of the integrate-and-fire neuron model: I. homogeneous synaptic input. *Biological cybernetics*, 95(1):1–19, 2006.

[8] Juan Luis Castro. Fuzzy logic controllers are universal approximators. *Systems, Man and Cybernetics, IEEE Transactions on*, 25(4):629–635, 1995.

[9] Teresa Ree Chay. Chaos in a three-variable model of an excitable cell. *Physica D: Nonlinear Phenomena*, 16(2):233–242, 1985.

[10] Teresa Ree Chay. Electrical bursting and intracellular ca2+ oscillations in excitable cell models. *Biological cybernetics*, 63(1):15–23, 1990.

[11] JOHN A Connor, DAVID Walter, and RUSSELL McKowN. Neural repetitive firing: modifications of the hodgkin-huxley axon suggested by experimental results from crustacean axons. *Biophysical Journal*, 18(1):81–102, 1977.

[12] Hugo De Garis, Chen Shuo, Ben Goertzel, and Lian Ruiting. A world survey of artificial brain projects, part i: Large-scale brain simulations. *Neurocomputing*, 74(1):3–29, 2010.

[13] Van der Pol B. The nonlinear theory of electrical oscillations. 1935.

[14] Mikael Djurfeldt, Mikael Lundqvist, Christopher Johansson, Martin Rehn, O Ekeberg, and Anders Lansner. Brain-scale simulation of the neocortex on the ibm blue gene/l supercomputer. *IBM Journal of Research and Development*, 52(1.2):31–41, 2008.

[15] Chris Eliasmith, Terrence C Stewart, Xuan Choo, Trevor Bekolay, Travis DeWolf, Charlie Tang, and Daniel Rasmussen. A large-scale model of the functioning brain. *science*, 338(6111):1202–1205, 2012.

[16] Richard FitzHugh. Impulses and physiological states in theoretical models of nerve membrane. *Biophysical journal*, 1(6):445–466, 1961.

[17] Erik Fransén and Anders Lansner. A model of cortical associative memory based on a horizontal network of connected columns. *Network: Computation in Neural Systems*, 9(2):235–264, 1998.

[18] Glenn Fung and Olvi L Mangasarian. Proximal support vector machine classifiers. In *Proceedings of the seventh ACM SIGKDD international conference on Knowledge discovery and data mining*, pages 77–86. ACM, 2001.

[19] Alexander RT Gepperth, Sven Rebhan, Stephan Hasler, and Jannik Fritsch. Biased competition in visual processing hierarchies: A learning approach using multiple cues. *Cognitive computation*, 3(1):146–166, 2011.

[20] CHARLES D Gilbert and TORSTEN N Wiesel. Clustered intrinsic connections in cat visual cortex. *The Journal of Neuroscience*, 3(5):1116–1133, 1983.

[21] Richard M. Golden. Stability and optimization analyses of the generalized brain-state-in-a-box neural network model. *Journal of Mathematical Psychology*, 37(2):282C298, 1993.

[22] David Golomb, John Guckenheimer, and Shay Gueron. Reduction of a channel-based model for a stomatogastric ganglion lp neuron. *Biological cybernetics*, 69(2):129–137, 1993.

[23] Haykin. *neural networks:a comprehensive foundation*. Prentive-Hall,Englewood cliffs, 2008.

[24] Simon Haykin. *Neural networks: a comprehensive foundation*. Prentice Hall PTR, 1994.

[25] Kaiming He, Jian Sun, and Xiaoou Tang. Single image haze removal using dark channel prior. *Pattern Analysis and Machine Intelligence, IEEE Transactions on*, 33(12):2341–2353, 2011.

[26] JL Hindmarsh and RM Rose. A model of neuronal bursting using three coupled first order differential equations. *Proceedings of the Royal society of London. Series B. Biological sciences*, 221(1222):87–102, 1984.

[27] G. E. Hinton. A fast learning algorithm for deep belief nets. *Trends in Cognitive Sciences*, 11(7):428–434, 2007.

[28] Geoffrey Hinton, Simon Osindero, and Yee-Whye Teh. A fast learning algorithm for deep belief nets. *Neural computation*, 18(7):1527–1554, 2006.

[29] Kaoru Hirota and Witold Pedrycz. Or/and neuron in modeling fuzzy set connectives. *Fuzzy Systems, IEEE Transactions on*, 2(2):151–161, 1994.

[30] AL Hodgkins and AF Huxley. Am j physiol london. *Am J Physiol London*, 117:500–544, 1952.

[31] Tank DW Hopfield JJ. Computing with neural circuits: a model. *Science*, 233(4764):625–633, 1986.

[32] Hong Hu and Zhongzhi Shi. The possibility of using simple neuron models to design brain-like computers. In *Advances in Brain Inspired Cognitive Systems*, pages 361–372. Springer, 2012.

[33] David H Hubel and Torsten N Wiesel. Stereoscopic vision in macaque monkey: cells sensitive to binocular depth in area 18 of the macaque monkey cortex. *Nature*, 225:41–42, 1970.

[34] W. Pedrycz K. Hirotao. A distributed model of fuzzy set operators. *Fuzzy Sets Syst*, 68:157–176, 1994.

[35] Anat Levin, Dani Lischinski, and Yair Weiss. A closed-form solution to natural image matting. *Pattern Analysis and Machine Intelligence, IEEE Transactions on*, 30(2):228–242, 2008.

[36] Hong-Xing Li and CL Philip Chen. The equivalence between fuzzy logic systems and feedforward neural networks. *Neural Networks, IEEE Transactions on*, 11(2):356–365, 2000.

[37] Hong-Xing Li and CL Philip Chen. The equivalence between fuzzy logic systems and feedforward neural networks. *Neural Networks, IEEE Transactions on*, 11(2):356–365, 2000.

[38] Su LI, Xianglin QI, Hong HU, and Yunjiu WANG. Synchronized oscillation in a modular neural network composed of columns. *Sci China Ser C-Life Sci*, 48(1):6–1, 2005.

[39] Zhaoping Li. A neural model of contour integration in the primary visual cortex. *Neural computation*, 10(4):903–940, 1998.

[40] Chin-Teng Lin and C. S. George Lee. Neural-network-based fuzzy logic control and decision system. *Computers, IEEE Transactions on*, 40(12):1320–1336, 1991.

[41] Tsau Young Lin. Granular computing on binary relations i: data mining and neighborhood systems. *Rough sets in knowledge discovery*, 1:107–121, 1998.

[42] Tsau Young Lin. Granular computing: Fuzzy logic and rough sets. In *Computing with Words in Information/Intelligent Systems 1*, pages 183–200. Springer, 1999.

[43] Tsau Young Lin. Granular computing: practices, theories, and future directions. In *Computational Complexity*, pages 1404–1420. Springer, 2012.

[44] TY Lin. Neighborhood systems: a qualitative theory for fuzzy and rough sets. *University of California, Berkeley*, 94720, 2007.

[45] Hongbing Liu, Shengwu Xiong, and Chang-an Wu. Hyperspherical granular computing classification algorithm based on fuzzy lattices. *Mathematical and Computer Modelling*, 2012.

[46] Catherine Morris and Harold Lecar. Voltage oscillations in the barnacle giant muscle fiber. *Biophysical journal*, 35(1):193–213, 1981.

[47] Vernon B Mountcastle. The columnar organization of the neocortex. *Brain*, 120(4):701–722, 1997.

[48] Jinichi Nagumo, S Arimoto, and S Yoshizawa. An active pulse transmission line simulating nerve axon. *Proceedings of the IRE*, 50(10):2061–2070, 1962.

[49] Timo Ojala, Matti Pietikäinen, and David Harwood. A comparative study of texture measures with classification based on featured distributions. *Pattern recognition*, 29(1):51–59, 1996.

[50] John O'Kusky and Marc Colonnier. A laminar analysis of the number of neurons, glia, and synapses in the visual cortex (area 17) of adult macaque monkeys. *Journal of Comparative Neurology*, 210(3):278–290, 1982.

[51] Adam Pedrycz, Kaoru Hirota, Witold Pedrycz, and Fangyan Dong. Granular representation and granular computing with fuzzy sets. *Fuzzy Sets and Systems*, 203:17–32, 2012.

[52] Witold Pedrycz and Fernando Gomide. *An introduction to fuzzy sets: analysis and design.* the MIT Press, 1998.

[53] Witold Pedrycz, Marek Reformat, and Kuwen Li. Or/and neurons and the development of interpretable logic models. *Neural Networks, IEEE Transactions on*, 17(3):636–658, 2006.

[54] Kathleen S Rockland and Jennifer S Lund. Intrinsic laminar lattice connections in primate visual cortex. *Journal of Comparative Neurology*, 216(3):303–318, 1983.

[55] Benyu Zhang Hong-Jiang Zhang Shuicheng Yan, Dong Xu. Graph embedding and extensions: A general framework for dimensionality reduction. *Pattern Analysis and Machine*, 29(1):40–51, 2007.

[56] Haijian Sun, Lin Liu, and Aike Guo. A neurocomputational model of figure-ground discrimination and target tracking. *Neural Networks, IEEE Transactions on*, 10(4):860–884, 1999.

[57] Shin'ichi Tamura and Masahiko Tateishi. Capabilities of a four-layered feedforward neural network: four layers versus three. *Neural Networks, IEEE Transactions on*, 8(2):251–255, 1997.

[58] Vladimir Vapnik, Esther Levin, and Yann Le Cun. Measuring the vc-dimension of a learning machine. *Neural Computation*, 6(5):851–876, 1994.

[59] Rüdiger von der Heydt, Hong Zhou, Howard S Friedman, et al. Representation of stereoscopic edges in monkey visual cortex. *Vision research*, 40(15):1955–1967, 2000.

[60] Hugh R Wilson and Jack D Cowan. Excitatory and inhibitory interactions in localized populations of model neurons. *Biophysical journal*, 12(1):1–24, 1972.

[61] Hugh R Wilson and Jack D Cowan. A mathematical theory of the functional dynamics of cortical and thalamic nervous tissue. *Kybernetik*, 13(2):55–80, 1973.

[62] Yi Yu Yao. On modeling data mining with granular computing. In *Computer Software and Applications Conference, 2001. COMPSAC 2001. 25th Annual International*, pages 638–643. IEEE, 2001.

[63] Yiyu Yao. Granular computing for data mining. In *Defense and Security Symposium*, pages 624105–624105. International Society for Optics and Photonics, 2006.

[64] Yiyu Yao and Xiaofei Deng. A granular computing paradigm for concept learning. In *Emerging Paradigms in Machine Learning*, pages 307–326. Springer, 2013.

[65] YY Yao. Relational interpretations of neighborhood operators and rough set approximation operators. *Information sciences*, 111(1):239–259, 1998.

[66] YY Yao. Granular computing using neighborhood systems. In *Advances in Soft Computing*, pages 539–553. Springer, 1999.

[67] YY Yao. Granular computing: basic issues and possible solutions. In *Proceedings of the 5th Joint Conference on Information Sciences*, volume 1, pages 186–189. Citeseer, 2000.

[68] YY Yao. Information granulation and rough set approximation. *International Journal of Intelligent Systems*, 16(1):87–104, 2001.

[69] Lotfi A Zadeh. Fuzzy sets. *Information and control*, 8(3):338–353, 1965.

[70] Lotfi A Zadeh. Toward a theory of fuzzy information granulation and its centrality in human reasoning and fuzzy logic. *Fuzzy sets and systems*, 90(2):111–127, 1997.

[71] Ling Zhang and Bo Zhang. Theory of fuzzy quotient space (methods of fuzzy granular computing). *Journal of software*, 14(4):770–776, 2003.

[72] Ling Zhang and Bo Zhang. The quotient space theory of problem solving. *Fundamenta Informaticae*, 59(2):287–298, 2004.

[73] Ling Zhang and Bo Zhang. The quotient space theory of problem solving. *Fundamenta Informaticae*, 59(2):287–298, 2004.

[74] Ling Zhang and Bo Zhang. Quotient space model based hierarchical machine learning. In *Neural Networks and Brain, 2005. ICNN&B'05. International Conference on*, volume 1, pages xiv–xiv. IEEE, 2005.

[75] Li Zhaoping. Pre–attentive segmentation and correspondence in stereo. *Philosophical Transactions of the Royal Society of London. Series B: Biological Sciences*, 357(1428):1877–1883, 2002.

Appendix

Associative Condition and Demorgan Law of q- Weighted Bounded Operator

It is easily to see $\oplus_f$ follows the associative condition and $x_1 \oplus_f x_2 \oplus_f x_3 ... \oplus_f x_n = \min(q, \sum_{1 \leq i \leq n} w_i x_i)$.

For $\otimes_f$, we can prove the associative condition is hold also. The proof is listed as below:

If $w_1 p_1 + w_2 p_2 - (w_1 + w_2 - 1)q \geq 0$, we have:

$$
\begin{aligned}
&(p_1 \otimes_f p_2) \otimes_f p_3 \\
&= F_{\otimes_f}(F_{\otimes_f}(p_1, p_2, w_1, w_2), p_3, 1, w_3) \\
&= F_{\otimes_f}(w_1 p_1 + w_2 p_2 - (w_1 + w_2 - 1)q, p_3, 1, w_3) \\
&= \max(0, w_1 p_1 + w_2 p_2 - (w_1 + w_2 - 1)q + w_3 p_3 - (1 + w_3 - 1)q) \\
&= \max(0, w_1 p_1 + w_2 p_2 + w_3 p_3 - (w_1 + w_2 + w_3 - 1)q)
\end{aligned}
\qquad ;
$$

if $w_1 p_1 + w_2 p_2 - (w_1 + w_2 - 1)q < 0$, we have

$$
\begin{aligned}
&(p_1 \otimes_f p_2) \otimes_f p_3 \\
&= F_{\otimes_f}(F_{\otimes_f}(p_1, p_2, w_1, w_2), p_3, 1, w_3) \\
&= F_{\otimes_f}(0, p_3, 1, w_3) \\
&= \max(0, 0 + w_3 p_3 - (1 + w_3 - 1)q) \\
&= \max(0, w_3 p_3 - w_3 q) \overset{for 0 \leq p_3 \leq q}{=} 0 \\
&= \max(0, w_1 p_1 + w_2 p_2 + w_3 p_3 - (w_1 + w_2 + w_3 - 1)q)
\end{aligned}
\qquad ;
$$

so $(p_1 \otimes_f p_2) \otimes_f p_3 = p_1 \otimes_f (p_2 \otimes_f p_3) = \max(0, w_1 p_1 + w_2 p_2 + w_3 p_3 - (w_1 + w_2 + w_3 - 1)q)$.

By inductive approach, we can prove that $\otimes_f$ also follows the associative condition and $x_1 \otimes_f x_2 \otimes_f x_3 ... \otimes_f x_n = \max(0, \sum_{1 \leq i \leq n} w_i x_i - (\sum_{1 \leq i \leq n} w_i - 1)q)$.

For more if we define $N(p) = q - p$ (usually, a negative weight w_i corresponds a N-norm), above weighted bounded operator $F(\oplus_f, \otimes_f)$ follows the Demorgan Law, i.e.

$$N(x_1 \oplus_f x_2 \oplus_f x_3 ... \oplus_f x_n)$$
$$= q - \min(q, \sum_{1 \leq i \leq n} w_i x_i)$$
$$= \max(0, q - \sum_{1 \leq i \leq n} w_i x_i)$$
$$= \max(0, \sum_{1 \leq i \leq n} w_i(q - x_i) - (\sum_{1 \leq i \leq n} w_i - 1)q)$$
$$= N(x_1) \otimes_f N(x_2) \otimes_f N(x_3) ... \otimes_f N(x_n).$$